NEW
TESTAMENT
EXPOSITION

NEW
TESTAMENT
EXPOSITION

*From Text
to Sermon*

Walter L. Liefeld

**Ministry
Resources
Library**

Zondervan Publishing House • Grand Rapids, MI

NEW TESTAMENT EXPOSITION:
FROM TEXT TO SERMON

Copyright © 1984 by the Zondervan Corporation
Grand Rapids, Michigan

Ministry Resources Library is an imprint of Zondervan Publishing House,
1415 Lake Drive, S.E., Grand Rapids, Michigan 49506

Library of Congress Cataloging in Publication Data

Liefeld, Walter L.
    New Testament exposition.

    Bibliography: p.
    1. Bible. N.T.—Homiletical use. I. Title.
BS2392.L54   1984   251   83-23419
ISBN 0-310-45910-9

Edited by Mark Hunt
Designed by Louise Bauer

Printed in the United States of America

83 84 85 86 87 88   10 9 8 7 6 5 4 3 2 1

To my wife, Olive,
who not only has a rich ministry of her own
and is my "fellow laborer,"
but who graciously tolerates my piles of books and papers
and the many hours spent with them instead of with her

Contents

PART III: APPLYING THE TEXT

Preface

This book is a product of my own pilgrimage. After years of preaching (from the waterfronts and street corners of New York to pulpits of many denominations) and years of teaching exegesis, I still felt that my sermons were lacking. What they needed was a kind of integration I only rarely saw modeled and never saw explained.

I am grateful to my students at Trinity Evangelical Divinity School, who were both patient subjects and perceptive critics as I worked out my ideas in class. Likewise the congregation at Arlington Countryside Chapel aided me by their honest responses to my messages during a number of expository series over the past years. Others have offered encouragement and often valuable criticisms, John R. W. Stott, Lloyd M. Perry, David L. Larsen, the unknown readers of my initial manuscript, and above all, Mark Hunt and Stanley N. Gundry of Zondervan.

I owe deep gratitude for the encouraging support of my children, David, Holly, and especially Beverly, who typed the manuscript.

PART I

INTRODUCTION

Chapter One

The Importance of Expository Preaching

What Is Expository Preaching?

Which of the following is an expository message?

Preacher Brown has chosen Galatians 2:20 as his text. He carefully deals with each phrase in the verse. Devoting approximately equal time to each major topic in his outline, he speaks of the crucifixion of self as the only way to spiritual victory, the importance of the resurrection power of Christ in our lives, the daily walk of faith, and the self-sacrificing love of Christ.

Preacher Gray was preaching through 1 Peter. The passage for the day was 1 Peter 3:13–22. He preached the gospel from verse 18 ("Christ died for sins once for all"). He dealt thoroughly with the issue of the "spirits in prison" in verse 19. From this verse he emphasized the certainty of judgment. Then he stressed the need for baptism as a means of identification with the death of Christ from verse 21.

Preacher Green was guest preacher in a church where, he felt, in the attempt to be relational and meet the personal needs of the congregation, the gospel tended to be neglected. He spoke on Romans 5:1–11. Rather than basing his sermon outline on the main clauses of the passage, he structured his sermon on subordinate clauses and phrases, such as "through faith" and "through our Lord Jesus Christ" in verse 1, "because God has poured out his love . . ." in verse 5, "while we were still sinners" in verse 8 and "if we were reconciled . . . through the death of his son" in verse 10.

Preacher White preached on the topic, "What Kind of Faith Works?" He picked up the thought from the end of Hebrews 10, especially verses 35–39 and then took most of his material from chapter 11. He selected examples that illustrated the kind of faith God sought in us, including examples from the list of those who suffered because of their faith in verses 32–38. He spent a large amount of time, proportionately, on the last two verses and also included the first three verses of chapter 12.

Which was an expository message? The first one, by Preacher Brown could have been, even though it concentrated on only one verse. However, he failed to take the context into account, which deals with justification by faith apart from the law. He missed the striking double use of the word, "law" in verse 19, which draws attention to itself as that to which we "die." He also neglected the following verse, which provides the conclusion to the passage. If he had faithfully studied that conclusion and observed the whole context, he would have seen that his sermon was actually a series of his own favorite thoughts on the spiritual life, which he impressed, wrongly, on this text.

Preacher Gray, in his sequence of sermons, had come up to one of the most difficult passages in the New Testament. Those of us who have tried to preach through a book sympathize with him. Such a passage cannot be avoided in a series. In his effort to deal with it, however, he got too deeply involved in the vexing issue of the identity of the spirits in prison. On the other hand, he failed to give an even exposition of the passage, and hastened too soon to apply its parts. In the process he imported his own views, true and important though they may have been, and failed to apply the passage in the same way Peter applied it in context.

Preacher Green seems to have committed the cardinal sin of emphasizing minor points and minimizing the main clauses of the passage. But Preacher Green had insight into the particular need of this congregation. They had already heard a great deal about peace and joy. What they needed was to know the *basis* of this in the death of Christ and the work of the Holy Spirit. In addition they needed to realize that all are sinners and none can claim peace and joy without repentance and faith. Preacher Green realized that these truths were basic to Romans 5, and applied them in a way that was faithful to the text. His message was, therefore, expository.

Since Preacher White gave a topical message, we might assume that it was not expository. Quite on the contrary, he understood the function of Hebrews 11 in its context and in the Book of Hebrews as a whole. Rather than simply preaching through the list of "heroes of faith," he anchored his message in the important statements that conclude the previous chapter. He also showed where this would lead by looking briefly at the beginning of chapter 12. In this way he also laid the foundation for the next sermon. But how could his topical sermon be called expository if it did not go through the chapter step by step? The reason is that his topic was drawn from the purpose and teaching of the passage. The theme is clear from the end of chapter 10. He did not impose a topic on the passage; he allowed the passage to determine the topic. Then he showed how the passage supported its own affirmation: the kind of faith that works is that which looks steadfastly to God and perseveres even in the absence of any visible support. The message was truly expository in that it explained the author's purpose and teachings in the chapter. It clarified the essential truths of the passage and prepared the way for the preacher to apply them in the contemporary situation of his congregation.

Expository preaching is an elusive ideal. Many preachers aspire to it, perhaps a good number feel they have attained to it, but in reality probably few are acknowledged masters. The examples above make clear that expository preaching is not some narrowly defined method of outlining the text. It is not just following a passage clause by clause. Likewise, a message can meticulously deal with details of vocabulary and grammar, and still fail to explain the intended teaching and application of the author. Our first task, therefore, is to determine the essential *nature* and *characteristics* of expository preaching.

Rather than commencing with a definition of expository preaching, we shall start with a consideration of *exposition* as a basic concept. The essence of exposition is *explanation*. If I explain something, I am reasonably free to choose my own method, but I must be faithful to my subject. If I were asked to explain the operation of a computer, I would not be at liberty to pick and choose certain aspects of it that particularly interest me. I would be responsible to explain, in proper balance, the basic elements of computer theory, construction, language, and operation. Unless I were giving a technical lecture on computer science, my talk would probably focus on operation, with only enough information on theory to make the operation understandable. Further, in a training session for operators, "operation" must include not only "how it works," but "how to work it."

Without a substantial content of clear explanation, balanced in its coverage of all major aspects, an exposition will be unreliable.

Without practical application, exposition is mere description. If exposition is explanation, expository preaching is explanation applied.

The essential *nature* of expository preaching, then, is preaching that explains a passage in such a way as to lead the congregation to a true and practical application of that passage. There is no single method by which this is accomplished, but are there any *characteristics* that are discernible in all true expository messages? We may suggest the following:

1. An expository message *deals with one basic passage of Scripture*. References to other Scriptures are always directly relevant to, illustrative of, and supportive of the teaching of the passage at hand. An expository message may also be a topical message, provided that it draws the essential information on the topic from one passage of Scripture. Reference to other Scriptures is subordinate to the exposition of the main passage.

2. An expository message has *hermeneutical integrity*. It is faithful to the text. This means that it reproduces the significant elements of the passage in the same balance and with the same intention as that of the original author. It does not omit or distort any essential of the message of that text, even to support true doctrines and good purposes. The text is not a box of candy from which one selects his favorite treats. It is the Word of God, which has come to us to be master, not servant. The sermon serves the text; it does not use it. If the sermon does not show awareness of, and respect for, the literary genre, original purpose, direction of narrative or of argument, and intended meaning and application of the text, it is not expository. That is the case no matter how much it may quote and refer to the passage. It is the case even if the individual message is part of a series on the book.

3. An expository message has *cohesion*. It is possible to provide many exegetical insights from such things as words and tenses, but yet fail to string the "gems" into a usable whole. Doctrinal truth may be brought out, ethical imperatives may be observed, but unless there is cohesion, the value of the parts is lost for the lack of a whole.

4. An expository message has *movement* and *direction*. An exposition may comprehensively deal with all the elements in a passage but fail to move the hearer in the direction intended by the biblical author. There are a number of ways in which an author can express such movement. Often subordinate clauses expressing,

for example, cause, effect, purpose, or comparison, will express this rather than the main clauses. Actually some of the author's main ideas are likely to be in the subordinate clauses. (Syntactical subordination does not necessarily mean subordination of ideas, since Greek authors often put some parts of long sentences into subordinate clauses for stylistic reasons.) Repetition of words and various expressions of emotion are, among others, ways movement and direction can be expressed.

5. An expository message has *application*, and that application will not violate the purpose, meaning, or function of the text in its original setting. Once again, without application, it is only exposition, not expository preaching. It is information, not a message. While the Spirit of God may be pleased to lead the congregation to an application even if the preacher fails to make it, the preacher dare not abdicate his responsibility to be God's spokesman, prophet, or evangelist.

Why Is Expository Preaching Important?

The most important aspect of expository preaching is that it conveys the biblical revelation of God and his will. Given the subjectivity of the preacher, the limitations of the human mind, the effect of sin on even our best thoughts, and the devastating effect of subjectivism on modern theology, it is more likely than not that a sermon will contain some error of fact or judgment. Therefore, the closer we stay to God's revealed Word, the less prone we will be to error. This is not to say that an expository message is the only valid kind of sermon. It is only to affirm that the closer we keep to Scripture in its own context, the less likely we are to err and the more sure is the declaration of God's truth. Nor is this to say that an expository message always expresses God's message for the situation. It is certainly possible to be insensitive to the need of the congregation or to the leading of the Spirit, and to give an exposition that may be accurate, but inappropriate to the situation or not properly applied. That is why the function and pastoral application of the passage receives special attention later in this book.

Another important aspect of expository preaching is that it teaches God's Word in the setting chosen by the Holy Spirit. Every Bible student knows that context is important. But context is difficult to observe and reproduce for the congregation unless we are giving a thorough exposition. Does this mean that I must choose between a topical and an expository message? No, for although the two are certainly different in their basic format, it is possible, as we shall see later, to build one or more "mini-expositions" into a topical outline. There is, of course, a danger in extracting principles or in quoting verses apart from their context to support my points ("prooftexting"). Deriving what is sometimes called a "timeless truth" or a principle ("principalizing") is an important way of applying Scripture to our current situation. But it is certainly possible, in our desire to make a contemporary application, to misrepresent the meaning of the original passage. Likewise prooftexts have their use, but we must be sure to preserve the meaning they had in their context. The New Testament writers often used prooftexts from the Old Testament independently of the context, but this was always under the special inspiration of the Holy Spirit. The Spirit who inspired the original text, and therefore knew his own intention, was able to keep the New Testament authors from misusing it. We, however, do not have that same inspiration and protection from human error, and therefore must use great care to observe the flow of thought expressed in its context. Therefore, while "principalizing" and "prooftexting" are, when properly used, valid methodologies, giving an exposition of a single passage is a more sure way than a topical message to present Scripture in accordance with its contextual intention.

A third importance of expository preaching is that it meets human needs. While it is true that an expository message can be accurate without being pastorally functional, God's Word is greater than the sermon. Given the weaknesses of the preacher, it is more likely that an explanation of a passage will speak to human needs than will a presentation of my observations on a topic. I believe that there is a valid application of Isaiah 55:11 here. The promise, which in its context relates to the proclamation of prophecy, is: ". . . my word . . . will accomplish what I desire and achieve the purpose for which I sent it." There is an implication here about the effectiveness of God's Word in producing the conditions of his kingdom, which may be compared with Romans 1:16, ". . . the gospel . . . is the power of God for the salvation of everyone who believes." Whether regarding the affairs of nations or the human heart, God's Word carries its own authority and power. There is absolutely no comparison between the effectiveness of even the best sermon and the Word of God itself. Therefore, the faithful exposition of God's Word is the surest way to meet the human need for that Word. A caution is necessary at this point, however. An ill chosen passage, thoughtlessly expounded by a preacher insensitive to pastoral needs, may not be the Word that God wants to use that day to accomplish his purposes. The passage quoted above from Isaiah does not guarantee that every Scripture read to a congregation is the one God will speak through. It says that God's Word is effective in accomplishing *his* desires and in achieving *his* purposes.

Fourth, expository preaching is important because it directs the attention of the hearer to the Bible. The purpose of the preacher should not be merely to meet a need on Sunday morning, but to equip the congregation to meet needs all during the week. He should not put himself in the place of the authority and resource, but should direct hearts and minds to the Lord. The Word of God itself should provide that authority and resource. The humble and wise pastor will show his congregation how to go to Scripture for him or herself, how to understand it, and how to apply it. We shall discuss further below the function of the preacher in modeling Bible study, but the point here is that an expository sermon is more likely to impress the congregation with the fact that God's Word, not the preacher, is their ultimate authority and resource.

Fifth, expository preaching is important because there is a great need, widely felt (if not consciously acknowledged), for the teaching of God's Word in a way that meets their true needs. God's people deserve better than superficial, trite messages. They are hungry for the true Bread. At the same time, there are congregations listening patiently to seminary graduates who are masters of exegesis and theology but do not know how to "put the cookies on the lowest shelf," so that all can share. The inability to serve the Word in bite-size portions only perpetuates the famine. Good expository preaching does not *impress* the congregation; it *feeds* them.

Finally, expository preaching can serve as an important protection against the improper interpretation of Scripture. For a number of reasons, such as a preacher's poor biblical training, faulty hermeneutics, and just plain laziness, to say nothing of deliberate distortion, many congregations today are subjected to fanciful and invalid interpretations of the text. "Spiritualizing" (drawing a spiritual lesson while ignoring the actual meaning of the passage) is so common as to be a plague. I suspect that as a result of poor modeling in the pulpit, thousands of Christians are "spiritualizing" the Bible during their daily devotions in an effort to "get a blessing" out of the passage of the day. Some devotional books also set a bad example in this. Calendars with Bible verses on them sometimes contribute as well, if they seek to bring some devotional thought from a verse isolated from its context. The place this trend can be best countered is in the pulpit, and the way to counter it is by expository preaching. The more closely the preacher keeps to the context, and the more carefully he preaches through an entire book, the less likely he is to "spiritualize" a verse. Spiritualizing can still be done, even in exposition, if the preacher ignores the truth-intention expressed in the context. But if he and his congregation are on their toes, it should quickly become evident, and the bad practice can be corrected.

What Are the Advantages of Expository Preaching?

In this section we will draw out some further implications from the comments above, and will add some practical observations. The difference between the previous section and this one is that the former is foundational to the very purpose of preaching, whereas what follows also includes what might be called matters of simple convenience for the preacher.

The first advantage is that we can be more confident of preaching God's will when we preach his Word. True exposition increases that confidence and the sense of authority that grows out of it. "Thus saith the Lord" is a traditional and often thunderous affirmation. It had better be accompanied by the faithful representation of what the Lord actually said!

The second advantage is a corollary of the first. In expository preaching we are confined to biblical truth. Subjectivism is minimized. The fear we all have (or should have) in ascending the pulpit lest we become spokesmen for error is minimized when we know that our sermon is a vehicle for God's true Word.

The third advantage is that as we preach through Scripture we proclaim the "whole counsel of God" rather than ride our favorite "hobby horses." Of course, we can always twist a passage, distorting or overemphasizing part of it in such a way as to misrepresent the true intent and emphasis of the whole passage. Assuming, though, that the exposition is faithful to the text, its context and its purpose, the sermon should be free from personal eccentricities.

Fourth, the context of a passage usually includes its own application. This provides direction as to how the passage should be applied today. This requires serious study of the circumstances that lie in the background of the passage, and of the flow of thought throughout the entire book, but this already is part of the task of the expositor. By allowing a passage to fulfill the same function today that it fulfilled in its original setting, we can avoid an awkward disjunction between the body of the sermon and the conclusion. We will not be at a loss as to how to make the passage "practical" if we already know how it functioned in its own life setting.

A fifth advantage is that Scripture often provides a literary structure that can form the basis for a sermon outline. Later on we shall learn how to observe not only the more obvious clause-by-clause flow of a passage, but also the "patterns" that, sometimes almost unnoticed, reflect the inner thoughts and feelings of the author. These "patterns" can provide excellent suggestions for sermon outlines.

A sixth and very helpful advantage of expository preaching is that we can include touchy subjects in the course of sequential exposition without being obtrusive. Every pastor knows how hard it is to deal with certain sensitive issues, especially if the congregation identifies them with certain members of the congregation. The tension can be lessened, if such matters are clearly part of the context that has been reached in the normal course of an expository series. Further, by handling such issues as they arise in a series, the preacher has a broader base than he otherwise would for dealing with them. He does not need to take extra time for orientation to the context, as this is already understood. If the subject matter is a case study of some biblical character, he may have already established a general portrait of the individual and explained the background circumstances and events. If the topic is an ethical or doctrinal matter, a basic theological framework is already in place. Consequently a sensitive issue can be treated much more thoroughly, and in the larger context of Scripture and theology.

Other advantages may come to mind, but the last we shall consider here is that expository preaching gives the preacher a fine opportunity to model Bible study. We have already observed that one reason expository preaching is important is because it directs the attention of the hearer to the Bible, rather than just to the preacher. But the congregation needs to know not only that Scripture "has the answer," but how to find that "answer" for themselves. If they leave church marveling at how much the preacher found in the text, they may never have the courage to seek the text themselves. But if the preacher shows them *how* he found his sermon points in the text, he may well be trading some easily dispensable mystique for a valuable teaching opportunity. If, in the process, he has to sacrifice some of the veneer of the sermon in order to expose the solid foundation, it is well worth it. Normally even that will not be necessary, for by following the flow of the text he may be producing a far better sermonic structure.

To expand a little further, I like to visualize a giant page of Scripture between me and the congregation. On my side is the text from which I prepared my message (ideally Greek). On their side is whatever translation the majority of the congregation is most likely to read. Even though I may have derived some of my points from the Greek text or a translation with which they are not familiar, I make certain that I draw attention to the corresponding rendition in their version. I think of my sermon as a dialogue, not between two, but between three: the congregation, myself, and the text. I try to address questions to the text, and to allow it, as it were, to speak for itself. As I move along in my sermon, I try to make clear (from my imaginary giant page of Scripture) just where I found my points and how I drew my conclusions. Far from destroying the pastor-people dialogue, it keeps us both conscious that it is God's voice through his Word that we both are hearing. If the preacher is obviously submissive to the authority of the text, and shows the congregation how to understand it by letting the sermon itself be a model, he has gone a long way to preparing God's people for their own life and ministry (Ephesians 4:11–13).

Dr. Paul White, the "Jungle Doctor," said some years ago that in the earlier days of missionary medicine in Africa, he found that it was useless to import Western type beds for the jungle hospital. The patients were not used to such beds, and when they returned home they would sleep in the same damp, unhealthy situations they had before. However, by using simple beds made of readily accessible wood and thongs, they were able to model for the patients a kind of bed they could make themselves. The patients would return home and by imitating the model improve their sleeping conditions. An expository message is a far better model for Bible study and for ascertaining the will of God for our personal lives than is the topical sermon or some complex type that does not grow simply and directly out of the biblical text. We all learn best by observing a good model. The preacher who uses time and energy to hold classes in Bible study methods (assuming he has that kind of concern), but fails to provide a model in the most natural setting at hand, his weekly messages, is hardly acting wisely or efficiently.

What Are the Goals of Expository Preaching?

Essentially the same as any preaching. This itself may come as a surprise, because there are some who think of exposition as appropriate mainly or even only in a teaching situation.

Expository preaching is an excellent means of evangelism. Many wrongly think that until a person becomes a believer, he or she should be given a heavy dose of the gospel, and the gospel only. To teach anything else may seem to be casting pearls before swine. This is an extremely short-sighted viewpoint. The more a person knows about Christian doctrine and life at the time of conversion, the further ahead he or she will be in the early days of Christian life. A good deal of the "follow-up" has already been done. Even more importantly, to preach the gospel in the context of exposition is to preach it more fully. The gospel is itself basic and simple. But it assumes a good deal of foundational truth. To preach passages that set forth the character and attributes of God, the person and work of Christ, the human condition and other doctrines certainly does not detract from the gospel. It prepares the way for the gospel, supports the gospel, and encompasses the gospel. One of the criticisms rightly leveled against some cults is that they lift Bible verses out of context.[1] This can best be countered by preaching the gospel *in* context. How foolish and impoverishing it is to preach Romans 3:23, "for all have sinned and fall short of the glory of God" (which is not even a complete sentence!) apart from its context about the righteousness of God, justification, redemption, propitiation, and the significance of the shed blood of Christ. That does not mean that one message should deal with each of these topics. It does mean that the fact of human guilt is only meaningful with reference to the other truths presented in that passage. Surely the gospel is presented more accurately and compellingly when it is presented in its fullness. One goal of expository preaching then, and one which is often neglected, is the preaching of the gospel.

Another goal is to minister to human needs. Somehow we have fallen into the logical fallacy of thinking that if a sermon is relational it cannot be expository, and vice versa. Quite to the contrary, it is when we separate a text or an idea from its biblical context that we incur the danger of also separating it from its real life setting. Without exception, every passage of Scripture has such a setting. It is not always obvious, and it may take some study of the religious and social background of the author's situation, that of the original readers (or hearers), and that of the figures and events in the Gospels and Acts to understand it. Even those passages that seem somewhat impersonal, as for example some of those in the Ephesian letter, which is not clearly tied to a local church situation, have a personal application. Failing to bring the congregation into the life setting of the passage, is a fault expositors can easily incur. For some reason it seems easier, or more proper, to abstract a principle than to help the congregation identify with a life situation or with a character in the first-century context of the New Testament and to make ethical decisions appropriate to her or his own life through that identification. Is not expository preaching, properly done, the best vehicle for helping our contemporaries find how God met the needs, and guided in the dark experiences of people "just like us" (James 5:17)?

Surely a related goal is to declare the will of God for his people, his church. But one of the greatest faults of us all is to seek that will in the isolated verse, perhaps arrived at by random. The underlying problem is that we fail to realize that the need for guidance towards a specific decision in our lives rarely exists in isolation. It is often coupled with a complex of events, with overarching ethical principles, and with our life goals. Frequently such a decision affects the lives of others. Our greatest need is to know the ways of God. That is, we need to know the character of God and the way in which he has, through the centuries, accomplished his will. Moses prayed, "Teach me your ways so I may know you and continue to find favor with you" (Exodus 33:13). John tells us that when Jesus and his disciples saw the thousands of people gathered to hear his teaching, Jesus asked Philip, "Where shall we buy bread for these people to eat?" Philip had been with the Lord Jesus long enough by then to have learned something about his "ways." He should have known what Jesus was capable of doing, what he had done in comparable circumstances of human need, and what sort of thing would be characteristic of him to do in that situation. The continual, faithful exposition of God's Word should also equip us in our day to make decisions based on our knowledge of the "ways" of God.

Other goals could be mentioned, and several more will be in sight when we look at the "function" of a passage in its biblical setting and today. In general, however, we might say that expository preaching should motivate us in such matters as faith, obedience, and spiritual growth. In what way does faith come from hearing (Romans 10:17)? In that context Paul has been speaking of the "word of faith" that is immediately available to us. It is not necessary to exercise great effort to reach God, for he has brought his saving Word close to us. Surely if we desire to stimulate faith or any other desirable response from hearts, the surest means is to bring the Word of God near. Conversely, when we explain Scripture, it should be with specific goals of spiritual response in mind. One of the common substitutes for expository preaching is what I call elsewhere mere description. It is possible to present a passage in an orderly accurate way, arousing great interest and appreciation on the part of the congregation, but in a totally aimless way. The sermon is concluded, the service ended, and the congregation leaves, unmotivated to change their lives in any way. That may be exposition, but it is not expository *preaching*.

When we think of goals in connection with expository preaching, we most naturally think of teaching doctrine or theology. The most common example is probably the restating of truths found in the Pauline Epistles. While it is the continuing task of the systematic theologian to synthesize the biblical truths and bring them into meaningful interaction with contemporary structures of thought, and while theology ought always to inform and correct our preaching, the best communication of divine truth is not always through propositions. By allowing the Scriptures to teach the truth in the context in which it was originally given, we also use a superb teaching method. In a sense, by teaching doctrine through expository preaching we are using a version of the case study method. Rather than making truth subjective by attempting to explain it in terms of contemporary life, is it not better to make it objective in the context of Scripture, and then apply it to contemporary life? God's Word *is* truth (John 17:17). What better way to teach truth than by teaching the Word! But again, it takes deliberate planning by the preacher to convey the truth enshrined in the passage to the congregation. Careless preparation may overlook not only nuances but bold statements concerning God and his world, not necessarily in propositional statements, but in other ways that are just as clear. Doctrinal teaching should always be in mind as a goal of expository preaching.

Our typical contemporary neglect of worship is reflected also in preaching. One goal of the sermon, and without doubt the highest one, should be the worship of God and the exaltation of his name. The sermon has a central place in Reformed worship. The proper kind of sermon can have a significant place in the worship of any Christian church. Unfortunately the sermon is so often concerned only with the human condition that its function as a means to worship is far in the background. A predecessor of this situation, if not its cause, is the lack of awe and reverence in the seminary study of theology. If God is only a topic in our seminary experience, God will only be a topic in our preaching. We fail to recognize the holy presence of God in his own Word only at great peril. The fatal experience of Uzzah, who touched the ark to steady it (2 Samuel 6:6–7), may have a lesson for us here. The Old Testament clearly teaches that God is known through his name and exalted through his name. I would suggest that there is a sense in which the Holy Scriptures are an unfolding of the name of God as they reveal his holy character and attributes. If my sermon does not "ascribe to the LORD the glory due his name" (Psalm 29:2) it has failed to fulfill its primary goal. Expository preaching should direct us to the Word; the Word should direct us to God. To be in the presence of God requires that we worship him.

What Are the Difficulties in Expository Preaching?

While some of the advantages mentioned earlier actually make expository preaching easier than other kinds (e.g., providing an outline ready-made in the passage), there is no doubt that this kind of preaching entails some unique difficulties.

Most obviously, it requires a thorough study of the passage. We are not at liberty to skim off some previously used verse, or to snatch a few favorite doctrines that we spy here and there. We are honor bound to work towards an understanding of the entire passage. We cannot neglect significant words, syntactical constructions, or doctrines. One of the final stages in organ building is "voicing" the pipes. Because of the different materials, sizes, and positions of the pipes, if left unadjusted they would be heard unequally. The skilled craftsman who finishes the installation therefore needs to voice the pipes to make them sound smooth and balanced. A sermon that lacks adequate preparation of all parts of the passage will come across unevenly. Not only some of the beauty, but worse, some of the truth may be distorted.

The difficulties of preparing a passage must not be exaggerated, but I suspect that many preachers put far too much needless work into preparation. I am convinced that the kind of exegetical instruction many seminary students have received leaves them thinking that exegetical preparation for sermons consists of parsing, diagramming, and doing word studies. Consequently, an inordinate amount of time is spent in detailed work, while the relatively more productive study of the passage in terms of its literary structure, flow of thought, and so on, is neglected. There is no surer way to discourage expository preaching in seminary courses than pedantry on the part of the teacher and drudgery on the part of the student. It is a goal of this book to bridge the gap between exegesis and homiletics. The gap is greater than it ought to be because of the limited, academic way in which many students learn their Greek exegesis. Suggestions to remedy the situation will come later in the book.

A second difficulty, related to the first, is the need to observe sound principles of hermeneutics. Actually, this should be done whatever kind of sermon one preaches, for any sermon includes (or should include) teaching from Scripture. However, if the sermon is expository, any hermeneutical failure can disable the entire presentation and result in preaching error. The preacher should have had a good course in hermeneutics in seminary. He must keep in mind what he has learned, review his textbook and notes, or, if he did not have a course as such, read at least one good book on hermeneutics before attempting exposition.[2]

Another related difficulty is that good exposition requires constant attention to the larger context of the book and even of the corpus (e.g., the Pauline writings). We need to be sure that we are properly representing the teaching of the writer and not drawing superficial and therefore wrong conclusions from a single passage. Similarly, the exposition of one of the Gospels will be enriched as I observe the particular contribution of that Gospel in comparison with the others. Redaction criticism can be of great help here. When we think of redaction criticism in its more critical form, i.e., looking for instances in which the Gospel author has distorted the tradition or added ideas of his own that are not part of the true tradition of Jesus' words and deeds, we naturally and rightly see little help (and many problems) for the preacher. But when we see and use it as a means of observing the unique perspective of each gospel writer on the person, teaching, and work of the Lord Jesus Christ, under the leading of the Holy Spirit, we have at hand a most valuable discipline for exposition.

The longer and more thoroughly a preacher has studied the entire New Testament, the more informed and rich his message should be. This does not mean that he will constantly refer to other passages. This can disturb the flow of the passage at hand, and give a poor model of Bible study. (Many Bible studies suffer from constant diversion to cross-references.) The wise and seasoned preacher knows how to weave the fabric of his sermon from the data of the passage at hand blended with matching strands from other relevant passages.

A fourth difficulty in expository preaching is that to be faithful to the original text it must be attentive to the literary form (narrative, parable, poetry, etc.) of the passage and its context. We shall see later how important this is. For now we may simply observe that there are times when the form, or genre, of a passage is part of the message. This is perhaps obvious when we are preaching a parable or other figure of speech, but it extends further. For example, before laying too much stress on the words of greeting, or of the opening prayer in a Pauline letter, we ought to know something about the literary conventions relating to letter writing in the first century. I say this not to discourage anyone from the task by implying that it takes an expert, but to encourage attention to the fact that the Bible is literature. Like any literature, it either follows or departs from the conventions of its day. Fortunately, good commentaries will explain such matters. My simple plea here is that we pay attention to such observations in the commentaries when they occur, and not dismiss them as merely academic. To know that Paul is transforming an ordinary epistolary convention into a distinctly Christian greeting (e.g., "Grace and peace to you from God our Father and the Lord Jesus Christ," Ephesians 1:2) tells us a great deal about the writer and his message.

The last difficulty to be mentioned at this point is that of matching the passage to the needs of the congregation. A topical preacher, who selects a fresh topic week by week is probably more likely to ponder the current pastoral needs of his congregation than the expository preacher whose topic is already fairly well limited by the next passage in a series. The remedy includes several ingredients. One is care initially in selecting the book itself, keeping in mind the various topics it will deal with. Another is to observe the function of each section in its original life setting. A third is to bear in mind that the same passage, while having only one basic interpretation exegetically, can be applied with integrity in various ways. Paul's prayer in Ephesians 3, for example, can be preached as an example of prayer, as doctrine, as a contribution to the flow of thought in Ephesians, or with specific regard to the personal needs it addresses, all without doing violence to the text or ignoring its basic meaning in that context. The preacher who is unwilling to carry the pastoral burden into his study will be a mere academician, not a healer of souls in the pulpit. The pastoral burden, like any burden, is, by definition, heavy. It is made no lighter by choice of the expository approach to preaching. On the contrary, the expositor needs to make himself even more conscious of that burden, lest he forget it.

What Expository Preaching Is *Not*

Undoubtedly there are many of us who share the fairly common esteem of expository preaching. We know that Bible-hungry people want it. Perhaps we have taken note that some of the largest attended churches are those whose pastors are expositors. We think of G. Campbell Morgan, Martin Lloyd-Jones, John R. W. Stott, and desire to emulate them. Somehow, however, we (and worse, our congregations) sense that something is lacking in our attempt at exposition. I recall one deservedly popular preacher who told his congregation one morning that his message was going to be expository. He spent no little time extolling expository preaching. But then he proceeded to preach what, in spite of its good intentions and many values, was little more than a collection of spiritual thoughts that he occasionally tied to verses within the passage. At the end, the hearer had little idea of the basic direction and teaching of the passage itself.

Sometimes our treatment of a passage is no more faithful to its meaning than that of some of the cults we criticize. It is only our evangelical convictions and doctrinal awareness that keep us from misusing the passage to the point of heresy. Sadly, this can happen even under the guise of exposition. Even more sadly, it can happen while we are under the apprehension that we are doing exposition because we have a passage open before us and are referring to it frequently during the sermon. Perhaps some examples will make things clearer.

Expository preaching is not verse-by-verse exegesis. Most students and preachers of the Word distinguish between exegesis and exposition. Some commentaries have separate sections for the two, although even in such cases there can be a serious blurring of the distinction. The difference is not simply that exposition may have some illustrations and concluding application. The whole package, wrappings and contents, is different. In exegesis, one studies each part of the Greek sentence, doing careful analysis with a view to understanding each truth presented accurately. In large measure this is done line by line. In exposition, on the other hand, the passage is studied as a whole, and with attention to the flow of thought or sequence of events. The function of the passage in its life setting is brought over against the life situation of the congregation. The needs of the congregation are held up before the passage to see what relevance its teaching may have to pastoral concerns. As we saw in the opening illustrations, a sermon may be truly expository even though it does not follow the sequence of the passage rigidly, as long as it explains and applies the text. On the contrary, a sermon may follow the sequence of the text woodenly and lead nowhere as far as pastoral application is concerned. Such a sermon is not expository. In earlier years (I hope no longer) I often did exegesis in the pulpit, in large measure because I was conscious of the deep and widespread hunger for teaching from God's Word. I finally realized that one can teach, but fail to feed or inspire. I think (and again hope) that my sermons today are no less informative but much more helpful.

Expository preaching is not simply a running commentary. By this I mean a loosely connected string of thoughts, occasionally tied to the passage, which lacks homiletical structure or appropriate application. It is less rigorous than either exegesis or exposition, and may ignore important aspects of the form, structure, semantics, and flow of the passage. Other comments above on verse-by-verse exegesis also apply here.

Expository preaching is not a captioned survey of a passage. By this I mean the typical: "1. Saul's Contention, 2. Saul's Conversion, 3. Saul's Commission" (Acts 9:1–19). In my own circles I think I have heard more sermons of this type than any other. They sound very biblical because they are based on a passage of Scripture. But their basic failure is that they tend to be descriptive rather than pastoral. They lack a clear goal or practical application. The congregation may be left without any true insights as to what the passage is really about, and without having received any clear teaching about God or themselves. Everything tends to be in the third person. I will refrain from comments on the alliteration! This kind of preaching can be useful in that it makes recollection easy. However, it can be too "cute" and draw attention to the preacher's ability rather than to the true intent and significance of Scripture. There are other dangers even more serious. The quest for a memorable outline can easily lead the preacher to ignore certain parts of the text simply because they do not fit easily into such an outline. There is a danger therefore of omission. Further, there is a danger of imbalance. The preacher may seize on a feature of the passage that is relatively subordinate and give it prominence because it lends itself to his outline, at the expense of some vital part of the passage that has the misfortune of not fitting his scheme. Yet another danger is that it may blind the preacher, and consequently hide from the congregation, certain important inner relationships of terms, ideas, doctrines, or other features of the passage. Such logical compositional elements as cause and effect can be lost completely in a captioned survey.

Homiletically, this kind of sermon may seem to be better than a verse-by-verse exegesis or running commentary, but it may not be. The example I gave above from Acts 9 is sterile. It does nothing to bring hearer and text into a vital relationship. The audience is nothing more than just that: an audience. They sit passively, listening to a verbal description of Paul's experience. That experience is one of the most vivid, exciting, and significant events of the New Testament, but unless its elements are applied pastorally, they will fail to teach, motivate, or have any real impact at all. The captioned survey, then, if merely descriptive, is neither good exposton nor good homiletics.

There is hardly need to go further in this catalog of marginal or substitute attempts at expository preaching. We could speak of two other types, at opposite poles from each other, and simply apply some of the observations given above. At the one extreme is the sermon that consists only of random comments on selected verses. This is the most subjective, lacking both the structure and authority of the passage as a whole, on the one hand, and the structure and communicative value of homiletic integrity, on the other. At the other extreme is the sermon outline that follows rigidly the main clauses of the passage. This may seem to be faithful to the passage, but, as we saw in the opening illustrations, it is possible that it misses some of the main *logical* points, which may not all be expressed in main clauses. Homiletically, it is possible that it is no better than the captioned survey if it fails in a pastoral way to bring life situation of Scripture and of congregation together.

The foregoing substitutes for expository preaching often share two basic faults. (1) They may fail to be faithful to the emphasis, doctrine, and function of the passage. (2) They may fail to possess the qualities that make for a homiletically sound and pastorally applied message.

How Can Expository Preaching Be Made Contemporary?

The question implies that it is not. This may lead to the inference that God's Word is not relevant. The cry for relevance in preaching has been heard for several decades now. Unfortunately there has been a reaction, and some preachers have been heard to say that God's Word does not need to be made relevant; it is relevant. Of course it is! But the New Testament is a first-century book, written in a language strange to Americans and coming from a Near Eastern culture. We do not experience the same background, environment, feelings, and so on of the original hearers of the Word.

There has been a great deal of study in recent years relating to the understanding of ancient texts. The principles of hermeneutics have been extended by new insights and even by new philosophical assumptions. We have been warned that it is all too easy for us to see Scripture through a grid of our own understanding. A good deal is being written on how far and in what directions we should go in adapting the biblical images and terminology to the cultural understanding of a particular country, tribe, or other people group today. The issues are complex, difficult enough for the student but almost impossible for one whose previous education did not include the recent philosophical, linguistic, and literary discussions on these matters.

Underneath much of the discussion is the idea that we cannot ever arrive at the true meaning of a text because our own "horizon" prevents us from achieving an undistorted perception of the "horizon" of the biblical writer.[3] "Horizon" in this sense expresses the limit to our perception and knowledge, much as the literal horizon marks the limit to our vision of the earth's surface. When a reader approaches a book that was written and read in a different time, language, and culture from his or her own, these "gaps" (to change the imagery for a moment), make it difficult to understand the message in the same way as the original hearers did. I do not subscribe to the idea that the task of "fusing" the biblical and contemporary "horizons" is so difficult as to make the attempt futile.

Actually, the expositor must also deal with the realities of different "horizons" even in his own day. We know that the word, "father," for example, means something quite different in, say, Africa, Germany, China, and the United States. Even within the same city the child of a minority family with a single parent may have a completely different perception and feeling about "father" from that of a white, upper middle-class child.

One might think that such gaps make expository preaching irrelevant and obstructive to pastoral communication. The fact is rather that good expository preaching helps bridge the gaps between the ancient Roman world and our own. It does this *provided that:* (1) the preacher is aware of the two cultures and the two horizons; (2) he has "done his homework" by learning all he can of the background and conceptual framework of the passage (even a brief look at a Bible dictionary or encyclopedia can provide valuable insights); (3) he takes into account the level of biblical knowledge, experience with Christianity and the evangelical subculture, educational level, and socio-cultural environment of his congregation; and (4) carefully takes the congregation into the life situation of the passage at hand before abstracting principles.

This task is not as hard for the expositor of the New Testament as it is for that of the Old, which is even farther removed in time and custom. However, apparent similarities can be deceiving. Anyone who has lived in Europe can testify as to the number of customs and perspectives that are unexpectedly different from those of the United States, though both are in the Western world. Perhaps our differing concepts of time provide a good example.

Once the differences are recognized, and one has "lived" in the biblical scene that is the setting of the passage under study, the preacher will need to analyze carefully and "feel" inwardly the meaning of the events, words (and more than words—semantic units, i.e., phrases, etc.), character delineations, teachings, and so forth in their setting. Then he will need to decide what most closely approximates to this in his own setting. This is the same route that must be taken by the person doing a dynamic translation of Scripture, or of any similar ancient work for that matter. Specific examples of this will be seen later in the book.

What, in Summary, Are the Characteristics of a Good Expository Message?

First, it conveys the basic message of a biblical passage faithfully.

Second, it communicates this message well, using a structure and features that are appropriate both to the passage and to the setting and goals of the sermon.

Third, it meets the real needs of the congregation in a way consistent with the purpose and function of the passage in its original life setting, and it is preached by a servant of God who is filled and inspired by his Spirit.

We may further simplify by identifying three concerns:

1. Hermeneutics (the biblical concern of the teacher)
2. Homiletics (the practical concern of the preacher)
3. Human Need (the personal concern of the pastor)

And the barest outline of the three would be:

1. Facts
2. Form
3. Function

Attempts at expository preaching that fall short do so in my observation because they lack one or more of these characteristics. They are like a two-legged stool, unstable at best, dangerous at worst. I am unaware of any book that attempts a balance between these three characteristics and that provides a good exegetical foundation that is useful to preachers whether or not they are at home in the Greek text.

To change the figure, the approach taken here can be compared to the Triborough Bridge in New York City. This bridge connects three "boroughs" of the city, Manhattan, the Bronx, and Queens. One can drive from any one to any of the others. So the preacher, during his preparation, should "drive" between the three aspects of fact, form, and function, constantly working on each one in balance with the other two. The end of the bridge we shall travel most heavily in this book is the exegetical, but the baggage picked up there will be constantly delivered to each of the other ends, the homiletical and the pastoral. We must keep the bridge open in all three directions if we are to be true teachers, capable preachers, and faithful pastors.

(Since I wrote this book, John R. W. Stott's book *Between Two Worlds* [Grand Rapids: Eerdmans, 1982] has appeared. It is a forceful presentation of the need and way to preach biblical truth to a twentieth-century audience. His fourth chapter deals directly with our concern here, "Preaching as Bridge-building.")

I have listed these three aspects in an order that concludes with "function," because we normally think of application as the final part of the sermon. For purposes of sermon preparation, however, the function of the biblical passage in its context and the application of the text to congregational needs should be considered *before* structuring the sermon. Therefore the order in the following pages of this book will be: facts, function, and form.

PART II

PREPARING THE TEXT

Chapter Two

The Facts: Practical Exegesis

Survey the Context

While we may be aware of the need to observe the context, some of us may need to enlarge our horizons regarding the *kind* of information we should be looking for in the context. We should also be aware that the social and religious background is also part of the "context."

Observe the Background

One of the most exciting areas of New Testament study today is the reconstruction of the social background of the Gospels and the Epistles. This study is far broader than earlier investigations, which have usually been limited to certain problem passages (e.g., women's headcoverings in 1 Corinthians 7). Recent studies range from attempts at reconstructing the social background that prompted the writing of the Gospels to studies on Paul and the issue of social strata at Corinth, to name just a few.[4] Such information will not only help to guide the interpretation of the passage, it will also provide excellent sermon illustrations. Many sermons are rich in contemporary illustrations (as they should be), but pathetically meager as to the life, events, tensions, emotions, personalities, issues, and other items that contribute to the background color of the New Testament. While the average preacher has little time or opportunity to read the most recent books and journals on these subjects, he can at least refer regularly to a good Bible encyclopedia or dictionary. A rich diversity of works is now available,[5] and failure to use these impoverishes both the preacher and his congregation.

Acts 16 provides a rich example of how background information might help. Geographically, Philippi was located on the way from Asia Minor to Greece. This is part of the transition in missionary work from East to West, and also the first major stop after Paul's vision of the "man of Macedonia" in Troas. It was a Roman colony and a leading city. It would have strong local customs, plus the individuality of a "colony" (in this case given special status when a large number of returning war veterans settled there). It had strong contacts with Rome itself. Paul was therefore vulnerable as a stranger and protected as a citizen. His insistence on certain rights as a Roman citizen was immediately honored (v. 37). There was no Jewish synagogue, a fact that perhaps reflects how few Jews were in that area, contrasted with most of the other cities Paul visited. Paul's major missions were conducted in cities with a large Jewish population, as well as commercial activity, good roads to other cities, and a garrison of Roman troops. Here, apparently there were not even ten men, the number required to form a synagogue. The women met for prayer outside the city gates. This was partly from custom and perhaps also because Romans kept cemeteries and foreign religious cults outside the city boundaries, since both were repulsive to them. This also says something about the reception Paul was likely to receive as a foreign missionary. Lydia was from Thyatira, a city famous for its purple dye. One gets the impression that she was an enterprising woman. She, like the jailer later in the chapter, quickly becomes a believer. Apparently her whole household (like the jailer's) responded. This was natural in a day when the household was a large unit (an "extended family" plus slaves and others) and tended to follow when the head of the household took a decisive step. (When we think of early Christian "house churches" we must not think of the small homes of today with only one or two parents and two or three children.)

The slave girl in the marketplace was engaged in a common and lucrative pursuit of those days, fortunetelling. There are many stories of such wandering soothsayers. She was a slave, as were many others (in Rome perhaps a third of the population were slaves). Her outcry was not supportive of Paul and Silas, as it might seem, but a warning against them. Her description sounds like Christian terminology to us, but such terms as "salvation" and "Most High God" were common among non-Christians. While what she said was true, it did not spring from personal faith but from demonic influence. The satirist, Lucian, provides insight into the practice of fortunetelling and its financial rewards in his "Alexander the False

Prophet." With the loss of this income after the exorcism of the slave girl, her owners brought Paul and Silas to the marketplace (the center of activity in an ancient city), to face the authorities. Because of the Roman *gravitas,* that sober dignity that made the Romans intolerant of immoral or ecstatic Eastern religions, and because of reverence for ancient laws and customs, including stable religious traditions, the local authorities were uneasy about foreign cults. This explains the charge, "These men are Jews, and are throwing our city into an uproar by advocating customs unlawful for us Romans to accept or practice" (vv. 20–21). Paul and Silas were thrown into prison after a flogging. The modern reader may wonder why there was no trial, and needs to be informed that in ancient times people could be jailed or put in dungeons without fair trial. It was not unusual for a ruler to put people away who were a threat to him (cf. Jeremiah and John the Baptist).

These observations illustrate a few kinds of information that can be gleaned about the setting of a passage. Much of this can be found in commentaries as well as in Bible dictionaries and encyclopedias. The more "stage scenery" the preacher provides, the more easily the congregation can identify with the biblical circumstances. The more we understand the religious and intellectual currents of a situation, the better we can understand and apply the biblical message to our own day. Once, when I was guest teacher of a large Sunday morning Bible class, I decided to see how well a passage could be taught by providing only the sort of background information given above for Acts 16. I asked the class to make their own contemporary spiritual and practical applications from this. The response was immediate and as good as many well-trained preachers could have done. Having "lived" in Philippi, identifying themselves with the experiences of Paul and Silas, they were perfectly able to make the application to their own situation.

Get a sense of the direction of thought. The importance of this was seen in the example from Galatians 2:20 in chapter 1. We have all heard messages on this verse that failed to convey the basic message of the passage. Paul is writing about justification in the larger context as well as in the immediate context. He is carefully working his way along, and in verses 11–16 has been discussing the issue as it pertains to Jews and Gentiles. In verses 17–19 he reaches a crucial point where the issues become sharply defined and the language becomes strong. In verse 19 the basic premise comes through clearly, and it is helped in the Greek text by repeating the word for law back to back in the middle of the clause, once in the genitive and once in the dative: διὰ νόμου νόμῳ. This is striking to anyone who observes the Greek text carefully, even if he or she has little or no knowledge of Greek. It is obvious to anyone who pays attention to the context and the direction of thought that Galatians 2:20 *must* be interpreted in terms of justification and the role of the law. This is reinforced in the following verse, verse 21.

Note the "Connective Tissue" Between the Text and Its Context

Taking Galatians 2 as an example again, we see that the significant ideas are indicated by *thought patterns* (the idea of justification), *verbal patterns* (the frequently repeated word, "law"), and a *structural pattern* (the juxtaposition of the words, νόμου νόμῳ, "through law to law"). Such patterns running through a passage and across the text chosen for preaching give a sense of direction like tire tracks across wet cement. Following the imprint provides continuity. These patterns function as a connective tissue that keeps the text from floating in isolation.

In contrast to the verbal pattern in Galatians 2, which serves to carry the *same* theme verse to verse, there is a pattern in James that serves to link passages with *successive* themes. This is a pattern not necessarily of key words but of catchwords. For example, the last word (in the original word order) in James 1:4 is "lacking" (λειπόμενοι). This serves as a catchword to introduce the next verse, "If any of you lacks (λείπεται) wisdom . . . ." Although this is a different type of pattern, it still helps us to follow the author's thought, and can be useful not only for interpretation but in structuring a message with reference to context.

Ephesians 1:10 provides another example of establishing a theme by observing repeated words and other patterns. What is the meaning and significance of the statement that God will "bring all things in heaven and earth together under one head, even Christ"? How does that fit in with the context? Why is it in the opening verses of an epistle which has as its apparent theme, the church? The student of Greek will also want to know how to understand the infinitive, ἀνακεφαλαιώσασθαι, "to bring . . . together under one head." Is it an infinitive of purpose or is it exepegetic, that is, explaining some previous word or phrase (perhaps here "the mystery of his will" in v. 9)? The best way to handle the text correctly in such a case is to examine the context for thought patterns, verbal patterns, and structural patterns. In doing so a very clear overall pattern emerges involving all three types. Integrally bound up with the summary of blessings in the first part of the chapter, and with the clustering of ideas around the Father (vv. 3–6), the Son (vv. 7–13), and the Holy Spirit (vv. 13–14), is the repeated idea of the *purpose* and *plan* of God. Note the following: "the will of God" (v. 1), "chose us . . . to be . . ." (v. 4), "predestined us to be . . ." (v. 5), "his pleasure and will" (v. 5), "to the praise of . . ."(v. 6), "wisdom and understanding" (v. 8), "the mystery of his will" (v. 9), "his good pleasure which he purposed" (v. 9), "when the times will have reached their fulfillment" (v. 10), "we were also chosen" (v. 11), "having been predestinated" (v. 11), "according to the plan" (v. 11), "who works out everything in conformity with the purpose of his will" (v. 11), "in order that" (v. 12), "might be for the praise . . ." (v. 12), "marked with a seal" (v. 13), "a deposit guaranteeing . . ." (v. 14), "to the praise of . . ." (v. 14). The verbal and structural patterns are even more apparent in the Greek, where there is an interesting repetition of forms, such as the repeated telic use of εἰς "for," or "with a view to" in verses 5–6, 12, 14.

With this pattern clearly before us, it is not hard to see that whether the infinitive in verse 10 is itself telic (purpose) or epegetic (explanatory; i.e., what is the "mystery of his will"), in this tightly woven context it has to express the climax of the purpose and plan of God. Christ is to be the acknowledged head of the universe. All that exists will be brought into meaningful relationship to and under Christ. A study of the verb, ἀνακεφαλαιόω, will reveal the great implications of that word. From this great climax in chapter 1, Paul will go on to show how the mission of the church includes its own submission to Christ, with all members of the church united under him. This unity, a "mystery" described in chapter 3, is observed even now by supernatural beings (3:10, which is followed by another series of terms having to do with purpose and plan). All this also explains the meaning of the "calling" of 4:1. Sermons on Ephesians should, therefore, show how the various parts of the epistle relate to the theme of God's purposes and plans in chapter 1.

Such patterns provide a "connective tissue" between passages in New Testament literature of differing genre. For example, in the Gospels, we need to find the meaning of parables in their own contexts. That means we need to see the connection between the extended metaphor of the parable and Jesus' direct teaching. In Luke 16, the parable of the unjust steward, or "shrewd manager" (the apt heading in the NIV text), is notoriously difficult to interpret. Since he is called "dishonest" at the conclusion rather than at the beginning of the story, it is possible to assume that his dishonesty consisted of his actions within the story itself. However the master does not call these actions dishonest but shrewd. The adjective, "dishonest" apparently has to do with whatever prompted his dismissal at the beginning of the story. But if he was dishonest at the outset, why was he not called so until the end? The answer is seen in a pattern of repetition. The Greek word for "dishonest," ἄδικος (v. 8), comes from the root, αδικ. This root occurs again in ἀδικίας ("unrighteous" [mammon, KJV], or "worldly" [wealth, NIV], v. 9), ἄδικος, "unjust" or "dishonest" (v. 10, twice), and ἀδίκω, again in the word for "mammon" or "wealth" (v. 11). The word, "dishonest" was, therefore, held in reserve until the end of the story to provide a "catchword." This catchword begins a verbal pattern that serves to connect the parable with its interpretation. Was the manager dishonest? We live in a world of dishonesty. Did he use clever means? We have at hand some means that can be used cleverly also, but these means are often considered tainted, or "worldly." The "people of the light" (v. 8) need to find shrewd ways to use this "worldly wealth," this "mammon of unrighteousness." The manager's money would soon be gone along with his job. Probably his home would be also, assuming that he was a steward or household manager, so he would need friends to welcome him "into their houses" (v. 4). Jesus carries over this general framework into the interpretation by referring to the time "when it [worldly wealth] is gone," and when we also will have new homes, the "eternal dwellings" (v. 9).

At this point, another pattern enters the picture. That is the repetition of words having to do with trustworthiness: "trusted" (πιστὸς, two times in v. 10), "trust" (πιστεύσει, v. 11), "trustworthy" (πιστοὶ, vv. 11, 12). Trustworthiness is as essential to good stewardship as is wise use of money. First Corinthians 4:2 says that stewards (managers) are required to be "faithful" (πιστὸς, the same word translated in Luke 16 as "trustworthy"). The manager in the present story, however, was not faithful; he was dishonest. Therefore trustworthiness here is the opposite of dishonesty. The two word patterns cluster around these two opposing qualities of dishonesty and trustworthiness. Christians are charged with being trustworthy with "someone else's [i.e., God's] property" (v. 12). Such patterns, once recognized, provide not only a key to the interpretation of a difficult parable, but provide a structure for a sermon as well.

This pattern is part of a larger one in chapter 16. The next section deals with values (cf. "valued" in v. 15, NIV) and with choice (v. 13). Once again, the theme relates to money ("The Pharisees . . . loved money . . ." is the only statement to that effect in Scripture). The following section contains the story of the rich man and Lazarus. This is connected to the foregoing by a third reference to wealth, the wealth the rich man lost when he died. A catchy topical outline of the chapter (though perhaps a little too "cute"), which ties together all these references to money, might be: "Use It" (vv. 1–12); "Don't Choose It" (vv. 13–18); "You'll Lose It" (vv. 19–31). Does such a topical outline distort the content? The answer must be, "Yes," if we are considering the teachings *within* each section, because other themes are included. However, the outline does not distort the *overall* pattern, because the thematic connection between the sections is found in the various attitudes people have toward wealth. Not only that, if Charles Talbert is right,[6] chapter 16 is part of a larger pattern Luke employs in this part of his gospel. This pattern (called a "chiasm") is one of a succession of themes, which are repeated in reverse order. To illustrate this by selecting only two of the alleged themes, we find "prayer" as a topic at the beginning of chapter 11:1–13; "possessions," 12:13–34 and repeated in chapter 16, and "prayer" again in chapter 18:1–8. It is interesting that in chapter 12, which is apparently parallel to chapter 16, we see the same general themes as we do in chapter 16, but in reverse order (i.e., also a "chiasm"). The topic, "You'll Lose It," third in chapter 16, can certainly be applied to the first section of chapter 12, the story of the rich fool (12:13–21), "Don't Choose It" can also describe 12:22–31 (e.g., ". . . do not set your heart on what you shall eat or drink . . . but seek his kingdom, and these things will be given to you as well"), and "Use It" is appropriate to verses 32–34 of chapter 12 (cf. "Sell your possessions and give to the poor," v. 33). While we must be careful not to strain at such patterns, when they are clearly present, we can make good use of them in preaching.

Note the Dominant Characteristics and Themes of the Passage

In the famous anecdote about the scientist Louis Agassiz, he was instructing a student about the importance of observation. After hours of painstaking notations on the details he had observed in a fish, the student had still not satisfied Agassiz that he had noticed everything important. Finally, so the story goes, the student exclaimed, "Of course—the fish is the same on both sides!" The preacher who studies very detailed patterns of words, syntax, and so on in a passage may be overlooking some obvious characteristics. At the same time, these characteristics may be very plain to his congregation. This may be especially true if the preacher is attracted to a few favorite themes that are emphasized in his denominational circle. A visitor to his church service, whose mind may not be in this groove, may see obvious phenomena in the text that are bypassed in the sermon. The result may be not only that important major themes are ignored, but that the hearer loses confidence in the preacher because he has apparently chosen to ignore them.

Ideas and Concepts

In the story of the rich man and Lazarus which concludes Luke 16, just discussed above, there are themes more important than the introductory topic of wealth. There are, for example, the Jewish concepts of life after death which the story reflects. The concept of torment is present, which is different from that of the Hellenistic world in which the story would be circulated. The idea of the fixed gulf, the presence of Abraham, and the elements of fire and water all call for attention. Most important of all, the concluding reference to one rising from the dead is of crucial significance, alluding as it does to the resurrection of Jesus. If the preacher merely preaches on the reversal of fortunes after the death of the rich man and Lazarus, or even on the unchangeable fate of one who rejects God, he misses the climax to the whole story, the obdurate refusal of people to acknowledge the resurrection of Christ and to grasp its significance regarding one's eternal destiny.

Doctrines

One might think doctrines would be obvious. However, the preacher may (for example) be so engrossed with the great topic of *faith* in his exposition of Romans 4 and 5 that he misses another corollary doctrine, that of *hope*. Paul introduces this, almost unnoticed, in 4:13 by describing Abraham as the "heir of the world." Then in 4:18 a verbal pattern, the placement of the phrases, "against all hope" and "in hope" in juxtaposition (παρ᾽ ἐλπίδα ἐπ᾽ ἐλπίδι) signals the reader that "hope" is a significant element in his teaching. Romans 5 picks this up (1) as part of a sequence in verse 2, (2) as the climax of a sequence in verse 4, and (3) as the main idea of verse 5. Although the word hope is not mentioned in verses 9ff., the idea is clearly present there also. The expository preacher will need to bring this doctrine out clearly if he is to be faithful to the text of Romans 4 and 5.

Character Delineation

Although biblical truth is often embodied in biblical characters, the expositor may, on occasion, look right past them. Acts 7 is of great importance for the doctrinal themes in Stephen's speech. What he says, however, about the refusal of God's people to obey him throughout the course of Old Testament history has even greater impact when contrasted with Stephen's own spiritual responsiveness, as seen in 6:5, 8 and 7:54–60. His true character also stands in contrast with the charges against him in 6:11. Many examples could be given of character delineation if we were to think of the various apostles, the members of the Herodian family, Pilate, and others. Personal characteristics are always important to observe when preaching from a narrative.

Sequence of Events

This may seem too obvious to mention, but that is just the problem. The sermon should not take the narrative, or the congregation's knowledge of it, for granted. For example, the perplexity of Herod the tetrarch (Herod Antipas) in Luke 9:7–9 is not just a sidelight; it is an important part of the narrative leading to Peter's great confession of Christ in 9:18–20. His question, "Who, then, is this?" significantly follows the same question asked by the disciples in 8:25, and the sending of the twelve in 9:1–6. Apparently the success of the twelve in preaching and healing makes Herod wonder whose power stands behind such marvels. The various speculations about a visitation by the deceased prophet Elijah, another one of the prophets, or the beheaded John is reflected later in the disciples' report to Jesus in verses 18f. Herod's question, "Who then is this. . . ?" sets the stage for Jesus' "Who do you say I am?" (9:20) and Peter's answer, "The Christ of God" (9:20). The event between these two scenes, the feeding of the five thousand, carries its own message about the Messiah. Therefore a true exposition of the great confession in Luke 9:18–22 will include the entire narrative sequence and, of course, include the following teachings about the Passion as well.

In the same way, the Transfiguration in Luke 9:28–36 must also be seen as part of this narrative sequence. In verses 18–26, there is teaching about (1) Jesus' identity, (2) his suffering, and (3) his coming glory. In Luke's narration of the Transfiguration these themes reappear in reverse order (another chiasm). The disciples first see his glory, then hear the discussion between Moses and Elijah about his impending suffering, and finally hear the voice confirm Jesus' identity.

Rhetorical Questions

Expositions of Romans 7 often founder on a failure to observe the setting of verses 14–25 within a sequence of the four rhetorical questions in chapters 6 and 7: "Shall we go on sinning so that grace may increase?" (6:1); "Shall we sin because we are not under law but under grace?" (6:15); "Is the law sin?" (7:7); "Did that which was good [the law] become death to me?" (7:13). When the expositor realizes that the discussion about our inability to obey God's law is in response to that last question, he will not subordinate the passage to some scheme of victorious living. Nor will he lose the attention of his congregation in a debate over whether Paul is speaking of his life before or after conversion. He will, in fidelity to the text, explain the purpose of the passage in its context with reference to the foregoing rhetorical question about the role of the law. Only then will he proceed to make the application to our spiritual life.

Complex of Topics, Problems, or Circumstances

The foregoing example of a rhetorical question also serves as an illustration of a complexity of topics or problems. In Romans 7:13–25 Paul is actually dealing with two matters at the same time: (1) clearing God's law of any suspicion of imperfection, and (2) sharing his own spiritual experience with respect to the law and to his sinful nature. We see this in the double ending to the chapter. The second aspect, which we might describe as personal, spiritual, and even emotional, is summarized first in 7:24: "What a wretched man I am! Who will rescue me from this body of death? Thanks be to God—through Jesus Christ our Lord!" The first and primary topic, God's law, receives its summary second, not in an emotional expression as with the other, but in a sober logical statement: "So then, I myself in my mind as a slave to God's law, but in my sinful nature a slave to the law of sin" (v. 25).

Another example of complexity, this time with respect to circumstances, is found in the Gospels. Mark 5:21–43 records the healing of Jairus's daughter and of a woman with a hemorrhage. The two incidents are intertwined, with attention turning from one to the other when the woman with the hemorrhage interrrupts Jesus on his way to Jairus's home. The reasons for such an intertwining are not clear to us. If it is simply because it happened that way, we can learn something about how Jesus handled an interruption, as well as about his popularity and his power. We also see a contrast between a woman with a chronic condition and a girl struck down in her childhood with a fatal illness. At a deeper level, we may be observing an instance when God in his providence allowed the interruption, delay, and consequent death of the child so as to permit an even greater miracle.

The opening chapters of Luke provide further examples of narrative complexity. There is a basic pattern of alternation here, with stories about the birth of John the Baptist and the birth of Jesus intertwined with each other. First, the angel foretells the birth of Jesus (1:26–38). Mary then visits Elizabeth, and the two stories come together in verses 39–45. Attention is immediately focused again on Jesus through Mary's *Magnificat* (vv. 46–56). This is followed by the birth of John the Baptist (vv. 57–66) and Zechariah's *Benedictus* (vv. 67–79). Chapter 2 opens with the birth of Jesus and continues with his infancy and boyhood. Chapter 3 tells of John's ministry, after which the narrative traces the life and ministry of Jesus. The preacher can use this literary structure (as the inspiring Spirit probably intended) to show not only the unfolding of salvation history but also to contrast the two figures of John and Jesus. Within this structure an interesting complex of circumstances appears in 1:5–23. While Zechariah enters the temple, "all the assembled worshipers [are] praying outside" (1:10).

We move from outside to inside, and observe Zechariah's visitation by an angel (vv. 11–20). Attention then turns again to the people waiting in suspense outside (v. 21). Finally Zechariah comes out, unable to speak to them (v. 23). This is a dramatic incident, and the expositor should allow it to have its impact in his sermon.

Other Features

Dominant themes are often signalled by inner patterns involving the sounds, meanings, or positions of words. Some of these will be observed when we discuss "patterns" below.

Select Significant Items for Exegetical Study

The preacher who has had the benefit of good courses in exegesis that are strong in syntax, textual criticism, and word studies faces a struggle of conscience every time he prepares a passage for preaching. He knows that each passage contains a gold mine of exegetical information. He has learned to weigh the moods and tenses, to ponder over the cases, to search the lexicons and theological dictionaries. Yet he also knows that pastoral visitation, committees, Bible classes, civic duties, and the proper needs of his family, along with unforeseen emergencies, will press in on him before another Sunday comes around. Should he take time to diagram that sentence in Colossians to be sure he understands it perfectly? Should he look up that verb in Hebrews 6 in Kittel[7] or in Colin Brown's *New International Dictionary of New Testament Theology*?[8] How much time should he spend in Blass-Debrunner-Funk,[9] or in volume 3 of Moulton,[10] or in Robertson's "big grammar"[11] trying to figure out what kind of infinitive Peter is using? Just as Paderewski knew when he hadn't practiced long enough, even if his audience didn't, so the faithful expositor may have a twinge of guilt if he has not invested hours of time in exegesis.

My advice is *not* to spend a great deal of time in these exegetical details *unless* (1) there are items in the text that are especially significant, (2) there is some complex pastoral situation requiring detailed, accurate application of the text, or (3) one has the (commendable) goal of sharpening his skills in exegesis, and pastoral demands are not pressing at the moment. But obviously some in-depth study is needed if the exposition is to be accurate and meaty. How, then, should we prepare exegetically?

The key question is, "What items in the passage are truly significant?" These items may be words or other semantic units, the uses of cases, moods, or tenses, or structural features (such as word order, along with clause and phrase relationships). Rarely will one need to repeat the labors of the textual critics, unless an alternate reading is mentioned as a footnote in the version commonly used by the congregation, or unless there is some great issue the congregation ought to know (see chapter 9). In such cases, a brief look at Bruce Metzger's *A Textual Commentary of the Greek New Testament*[12] is usually sufficient. If we are to spend time only on matters of significance, we will need some criteria for selecting these. I propose the following:

Doctrinally Important

It would be unthinkable to gloss over the word "image" in Colossians 1:15 or "righteousness" in Romans 3. Likewise, the prepositional phrase, "in accordance with the Spirit" in Romans 8 and the word "grace" in Ephesians 2:8 call for careful study, because they are doctrinally important and essential to the understanding of the passage in which they occur. Further examples are hardly necessary. There are always some words or constructions that are more central than others to the meaning of a passage.

Ethically Important

The meaning of "foolish talk" in Ephesians 5:4 needs to be understood if the congregation is to refrain from it. The different tenses used for the word "present" (or "offer") in Romans 6:13 may be important for the person seeking help in the spiritual life. Consideration of the meaning of the words "deeply moved" and "troubled," describing Jesus' emotions in John 11:33, may help some who feel guilty over their own feelings of emotion. There is much confusion over the meaning and application of the words "old self" (or "man") and "new self" (or "man") in Ephesians 4:22–24 and Colossians 3:9–10.

Difficult to Understand

This is probably the single greatest cause for exegetical research. The danger, especially in courses on exegesis, is that we become so "problem centered" that we fail to learn how to use exegesis in a positive way. Nevertheless there are many times when a passage is obscure and requires thorough study. A classic example is 1 Peter 3:18–22. We may use this here to show the various kinds of study that a difficult text requires. For example, what kind of dative is πνεύματι? Does it mean "in" or "by" the "spirit" (small "s") or "Spirit" (capital "S")? The juxtaposition of the phrases θανατωθεὶς μὲν σαρκὶ ("put to death in the body") and ζωοποιηθεὶς δὲ πνεύματι ("but made alive by the Spirit") is significant. So is the participle πορευθεὶς ("when he went"...where?), and the troublesome phrase, "spirits in prison."

When we meet a passage with difficult words or constructions such as these, we need to weigh carefully how much original research or commentary reading we ought to do. But our decision should not merely rest on whether we find it difficult or interesting ourselves. It is perhaps even more important to be aware of passages that the *congregation* will find difficult. It is probably trite to say this, but we need to keep in mind that the well-educated preacher will find some problems pressing or fascinating for himself, but which mean virtually nothing to his congregation, while on their part they struggle with other matters he has long since settled. Once again the preacher needs to be a thoughtful pastor, or he will find his sermons to be far from where the congregation really is.

Thematic in the Context, Book, or Corpus

The word, "people," may not seem especially important doctrinally or ethically, and it certainly is not difficult to understand. Yet it is one of the significant words in the Gospel of Luke. To ignore it in a passage may mean that our sermon will fail to convey an important truth. Luke is very careful to distinguish between the "people"(λαός), the "crowds" (ὄχλος), the various leaders and, of course, the disciples. The "crowds" are uncommitted, sometimes brusque or hostile. The leaders from the beginning are suspicious and eventually openly antagonistic. The "people," however, are open to Jesus' teaching. They are pious, ready to believe and to follow Jesus (e.g., Luke 1:17, 68, 77; 2:10, 31–32; 7:16; 19:47, 48; 20:1; 21:38; 24:19). The significance of this word can be seen not only in specific occurrences, but in the fact that Luke uses it over thirty-five times, in contrast to Mark's mere three uses.

Crucial to an Understanding of the Author's Intent

Perhaps the best example is from the great christological passage, Philippians 2:6–11. The words, "made himself nothing" (KJV: "emptied himself"), in verse 7 cry out for some clear explanation. A serious doctrinal issue hangs on our understanding of this phrase. Therefore the expositor will carefully study the modifying clause that follows, "taking the very nature of a servant." He must understand, and convey to the congregation, the way that clause explains the meaning of the preceding words about Jesus' "kenosis" or self-emptying.

Dependent on the Literary Form

The figurative use of Sarah and Hagar in Galatians 4:21–31 requires very careful treatment. There are well-known parts of the Book of Revelation for which accurate determination of literary form is crucial. The parables of Jesus provide another obvious illustration. The interpreter of the story of the rich man and Lazarus in Luke 16 needs to be extremely careful as to how he handles the elements of that story.

Chapter Three # The Facts:
Exegetical Outlines

Prepare a Paragraph Outline of the Passage

Paragraph outlines are a helpful device that has been in use for some years now. Many have learned it from Merrill C. Tenney's book on Galatians, in which he exhibited different methodologies for Bible study.[13] He called it the "Analytical Method." In this analysis, the main clauses in the paragraph are written out beginning at the left-hand margins. Subordinate constructions are indented under these. Tenney also used this method to lay out interesting structures, e.g.,

> For the flesh lusteth against the Spirit,
> and the Spirit   against the flesh;

Following the analysis, he constructed an outline that followed its features. In doing this, he allowed some flexibility. For example, he did not insist on turning every main clause *per se* into a main point in the sermon. Greek syntax is too subtle to be handled that way. He sought rather to convey the basic thoughts in his sermonic points.

Obviously, the expositor will find this method useful because it will help him to give proper attention to the major affirmations of the biblical text in his sermon, and also to devote the divisions of his sermon to the successive parts of the text in due proportion. Because it is easy for us to be drawn to a few points that are important to us, we need some objective way of insuring our attention to the entire passage and its major teachings. Also, for many passages, it is the paragraph outline that will provide the best outline for a message. There are some exceptions and limitations to this, as we shall see shortly.

The first step is to determine the natural limits of the passage. This is done by observing both the syntax and the content. As we have observed above, there are various types of "connective tissue" in the text, so that it is difficult (and wrong) to isolate a passage completely from its context. However, there are transitions of thought to be noted, and these are indicated by certain marks. In the Greek syntax, such a new beginning is sometimes, though not often, indicated by the absence of a conjunction. The new paragraph may introduce new concepts with a description or definition. For a classic example, Romans 1:16–17 is both dependent on its context and, at the same time, significant in itself. It begins *"For I am not ashamed..."* (οὐ γὰρ ἐπαισχύνομαι), the conjunction clearly linking it with the foregoing paragraph. At the same time, the word, "righteousness" (δικαιοσύνη) appears without an article. This is probably because Paul is stressing the unique quality of God's righteousness, but also because the concept has not previously appeared in his discussion. The same phenomenon appears in the following paragraph, which opens with a phrase containing the anarthrous ὀργὴ θεοῦ, "wrath of God." With each new concept, the discussion takes a major turn. Of course, our Greek texts and English translations have already divided the material into verses and paragraphs. We should keep in mind the translation most of the congregation will be using and follow the chapter divisions they see. (Remember my earlier suggestion about imagining a giant page of Scripture between the preacher and the congregation.) Even so, we should be aware ourselves of the *reasons* for the English paragraph divisions, because this will make us more sensitive to the flow of the text. Also, on rare occasions, we may need to disagree with those divisions with which the congregation is familiar, and we need to be able to do this with understanding and clarity.

After we have decided on the limits of the passage that will form the basis of our sermon, we will look for the main affirmations. These will usually appear as main clauses. Therefore we will do best to focus on those main clauses, even if we need to make some modifications later on. We will list the main clauses and, indented under them, the subordinate clauses and modifying phrases as shown in the diagrams below. Note that wherever possible, a modifying phrase begins under the word it modifies.

It is best not to be too technical in this diagram, since its purpose is to provide a clear outline for the sermon, simplified for better understanding and retention. However, it must be accurate, so that we do not teach error. Part of the process of simplification is to realize that some clauses, even though syntactically structured as main clauses, actually function to modify or expand the idea of other clauses. These should be indented, like subordinate constructions, under the clauses they explain. This may mean that the sermon outline will pick up a main clause only every several lines or so. If this follows the intended sense of the passage, it is not a distortion, but a clarification. We shall see later that all subordinate clauses, all phrases, and all main clauses that have been indented need to be examined for possible major doctrinal or ethical input. For the first paragraph outline, however, we will put at the margin only main clauses that are clearly intended to mark the major affirmations.

Another step in simplification, especially if the passage chosen is long, may be to select only those main clauses that mark a transition in thought. I will provide examples from Matthew 6 and 7 later on.

Here is an obvious example from Colossians 1:15–20. For this initial example I am using English, and am not including all the subordinate material. For this reason, it will be well to have the full text, preferably in Greek, open before you. I shall treat the initial relative clause as a main clause, because that is its sense, the use of the relative possibly reflecting an original creedal form.

v. 15   Who is the image of the invisible God,
        [and is] the firstborn over all creation.
v. 16   For by him all things were created:
                    things in heaven (etc.). . .
v. 17   He is before all things
        and in him all things hold together.
v. 18   And he is the head of the body, the church;
        he is the beginning
        (he is) the firstborn from among the dead,
                so that in everything he might have the supremacy.
            For (Greek, "because") God was pleased
                to have all his fullness dwell in him,
                and through him to reconcile . . . all things . . . .

We thus have a series of affirmations about Christ, all expressed (with the exception of the creedal "who" in v. 15) in main clauses. For the sermon itself we would probably divide these between the relation of Christ to God, to the universe, and to the church. Also, in a sermon outline, we will probably want to take the purpose clause in verse 19, "so that in everything he might have the supremacy," as the major topic, as follows:

Why should Jesus have the supremacy?
  1. Because of his relationship to God
        "He is the image of the invisible God"
  2. Because of his relationship to the universe
        "For by him all things were created"
        "He is before all things"
        "In him all things hold together"
  3. Because of his relationship to the church
        "He is the head of the body, the church"
        "He is the beginning"
        "He is the firstborn from among the dead"

At this point, we may want to look again at verses 19–20. The words, "For God was pleased to have all his fullness dwell in him," are a causal clause, explaining why Jesus should have the supremacy. Therefore, even though they do not constitute a main clause in Greek, they perform the same *function* as the affirmations that we have already turned into causal clauses in our sermon outline above! So we can add point 4:

  4. Because of his relationship to God's plan
        "For God was pleased . . .
            to have all his fullness dwell in him
            to reconcile, through him, all things . . ."

That last point, "Because of his relationship to God's plan," may seem a little strained. It illustrates the problem common to all sermon preparation, of reworking biblical expressions into consistent English headings. Perhaps in this case we could do better, but the important thing is that we retain the *causal idea*, because that is what the Greek text has. In summary, the first series of affirmations lead to a purpose clause, "so that . . . supremacy," which, in turn is followed by a causal clause. We have simply made the purpose clause the major topic, and have listed the affirmations and the causal clause as reasons for acknowledging Jesus' supremacy. This conveys precisely the intent of the Greek structure. This is still not a sermon, but it is a skeleton outline with which to begin.

Here is another example, this time from Colossians 3:1–17.

v. 1   Since, then, you have been raised with Christ,
          set your hearts on things above
                              where Christ is seated . . . .
v. 2   Set your minds on things above,
                    not on earthly things
v. 3   For you died,
          and your life is now hidden with Christ in God.
v. 4   When Christ,   appears,
               who is your life,
          then you also will appear with him . . .
v. 5   Put to death, therefore . . .
               [subordinate phrases]
v. 8   Put off now . . .
               [subordinate phrases]
v. 12 Put on . . .
               [subordinate phrases]
v. 16 Let the word of Christ dwell in you richly . . .
               [subordinate phrases]

Even such a simple example as the above raises a number of questions. Why did we start with Colossians 3:1? The words "Since you have been raised with Christ" have an earlier parallel in 2:20: "since you died with Christ." The expositor will have to decide whether to include that parallel. To be faithful to the text and to the theological-ethical integrity of the passage he should include it. The preacher may object that this will make for an imbalanced sermon, as far as the length of its divisions is concerned. In this case he may have to choose between form and truth. There is another possibility, of course. If he includes 2:20–23 with the rest of chapter 2 (or at least with its latter part), he will draw the congregation's attention to the parallel between 3:1 and 2:20 both when he preaches on chapter 2 and again when he preaches on chapter 3.

Another problem relates to 3:15, "Let the peace of Christ rule in your hearts." If the main verbs are imperatives, and if "rule" is also an imperative, does it not belong in the series? In both the English translation and Greek clause structure it seems to be in parallel to "Let the word of Christ dwell in you richly" (v. 16). To include verse 15 certainly would not be wrong, and, in fact, might be preferable. Why, then, is it omitted in the outline above? First, it does not really introduce a new topic, but summarizes what Paul has been saying about "putting on" Christian virtues. He has been speaking of such qualities as compassion, kindness, and, in verse 14, love, as a means of unity. In spite of the typical paragraph division in the English translations, which makes verse 15 the beginning of a new paragraph, it actually concludes the previous one. The true new beginning is "let the word of Christ dwell . . . ," and the key to this is the absence of a conjunction to introduce it. Another clue is that verses 16–17 are in parallel to the verses in Ephesians 5:18–21 about the filling of the Spirit and its effects. Clearly this is a major topic in Paul's mind and calls for separate attention, whereas the previous saying about the peace of Christ is part of another topic.

I have deliberately included a discussion on such a matter of opinion to show that even that basic paragraph outline is not a mechanical procedure. The expositor is constantly forced back to the text. Even if in the end it does not matter how "Let the peace of Christ rule . . ." is placed in the outline, by the time the outline is completed the expositor will have thought through the structure of the passage, and his sermon will be the richer for it.

A final question is, why, when the paragraphs covered in the outline seem to contain, at least in English translation, a number of main clauses, did we not reflect these in the outline? First, what appear as main clauses in English are often subordinate in Greek. They are translated as independent clauses to simplify the rather cumbersome and complex Greek syntax. Second, there is a pattern, which is perhaps more evident in the Greek than in the English text, of a sequence of imperatives. When we come to the discussion of patterns, we shall see that there are occasions when a pattern is a better guide to a sermon outline than a paragraph analysis, or, at least, when a pattern should be allowed to modify the paragraph analysis.

We shall now look at another sample, from Romans 5:1–11. At the right margin I have described the function of each successive clause and phrase. These are simple "homemade" descriptions. They do not follow any formal grammatical categories. You can invent your own descriptive words. The purpose is to force oneself to observe the relationship of the various parts of a sentence to each other. Our understanding of these relationships can then be brought into the sermon as we explain where, when, how, under what conditions, and so on, the main affirmations are true or applicable. This takes discipline, but it pays off in a faithful exposition of the passage.

Romans 5:1-11

Therefore	CONSEQUENCE
since we have been justified	GROUND
by faith	MEANS
we have peace with God	AFFIRMATION
through our Lord Jesus Christ	AGENT
through whom . . . access	AGENT
by faith	MEANS
into this grace	LOCATION
in which . . . stand	LOCATION
we rejoice in the hope of the glory of God	AFFIRMATION
Not only so	CONTRASTING
We rejoice in our sufferings	AFFIRMATION
because we know	CAUSE
that suffering produces perseverance	
persev. [”] character	
charac. [”] hope	
Hope does not disappoint us	AFFIRMATION
because God has poured out his love	CAUSE
into our hearts	LOCATION
by the Holy Spirit	AGENT
whom he has given us	IDENTIFICATION
At just the right time	TIME
when we were still powerless	TIME
Christ died for the ungodly	AFFIRMATION
(For) one rarely dies for a righteous person	ASSUMPTION
(For) one possibly may die for a good person	ASSUMPTION
But God demonstrates his love for us	AFFIRMATION
in that↓	
while we were yet sinners	TIME
Christ died for us	EXPLANATION
Since we have now been justified . . .	GROUND
how much more	COMPARATIVE
. . . shall we be saved	AFFIRMATION
from God's wrath	SEPARATION
through him	AGENT
For if we were reconciled to him . . .	CONDITION
by the death of his Son	AGENT
when we were enemies	TIME
how much more	COMPARATIVE
. . . shall we be saved	AFFIRMATION
by his life	MEANS
Not only is this so	CONTINUATION

but we also rejoice in God	AFFIRMATION
through our Lord Jesus Christ	AGENT
through whom . . .	AGENT
. . . reconciliation	

To help in the identification of main and subordinate clauses, here is a partial list of conjunctions that introduce the two types. Coordinating conjunctions include: and, but, therefore, moreover, however, yet. Subordinating conjunctions include: because, although, so that, whether, since, while, when, until, where, in order that. One difficult word to classify is "for" (often representing the Greek γάϱ). It can mean "because," in which case it introduces a subordinate concept (even though γάϱ does not grammatically introduce a subordinate clause). Otherwise it simply continues the thought, possibly adding an inference ("So then . . .") or an explanation ("You see . . .").

Some of the common Greek coordinating conjunctions are: ἀλλά, ἄρα, γάϱ, δέ, διό, εἴτε...εἴτε, ἤ, καί, μέν, μέντοι, οὖν, οὐδέ, μή, μηδέ, οὔτε, πλήν, τέ. Some of the subordinating conjunctions are: ἄχϱη, διότι, ἐάν, εἰ, ἐπεί, ἐπειδή, ἕως, ἵνα, κάθαπεϱ, καθώς, καίπεϱ, μεχϱί, μή (in certain constructions), μήποτε, μήπως, ὅπως ὅτε, ὅτι, πρίν, ὡς, ὥσπεϱ, ὥστε.

When reading a phrase in English, be sure that the word in question is indeed a conjunction and not a preposition. A preposition introduces a word, as in "before the judge." A conjunction introduces a whole clause: "before he crossed the street."

Prepare a Structural Outline

A survey of the primary affirmations shows a clear sequence in Paul's mind:

1. We have *peace* (v. 1)
2. We rejoice in *hope* (v. 2)
3. We rejoice in *sufferings* (which produce *hope*, vv. 3–4)
4. *Hope* does not disappoint us (because we are certain of God's *love*, vv. 5–6, which love is evidenced by the *cross* and its effects, vv. 7–10)

It is necessary at this point to anticipate our later discussion on "patterns," because the relationship of the main affirmations is seen clearly only when certain patterns are observed.

Verses 1 and 11 illustrate the pattern of "equivalents." This feature is marked by the repetition of certain words (or phrases or morphemes) and the substitution of others. Observe the following:

(v. 1)   We have peace .... through our Lord Jesus Christ, through whom we have access ...

(v. 11) We rejoice in God .... through our Lord Jesus Christ, through whom we have now received ...

But note that verse 11 also shares in another construction of equivalents:

(v. 2)   We rejoice in ... hope
(v. 3)   We rejoice in ... sufferings
(v. 11) We rejoice in ... God

Therefore, verse 11 is connected both with verse 1 and with verses 2 and 3 by means of this feature. Emphasis is on the benefits of justification (we have peace and we have joy) and on the objects of our rejoicing (hope, suffering, and God himself).

The idea of hope is expressed both directly, as one of the benefits of justification, and indirectly, as the outcome of our sufferings. Therefore, the sufferings alone are not a primary object of our joy, but insofar as they lead to hope. We may want to rethink the matter of listing "We rejoice in sufferings" as a main affirmation, but we dare not remove it very far from the major headings.

Further, Paul makes it clear that the reason hope does not disappoint us is because it has an objective basis in God's love, which he has poured into our hearts by the Spirit. That love, in turn, is absolutely certain because we can look back in history and recall that Christ died, not for good people, but for bad ones, ourselves. We stand in between the past, when Christ died, and the future, which is made sure by that historical death. Therefore in the present time, we have an objectively grounded hope. But how does this affect the listing of the clauses? There are some main *clauses* in verses 7–10, but they are *not* among the main *affirmations,* which are a list of the benefits of justification. Rather they serve to *support* one of those affirmations, namely, that we have a firm hope even when that hope may seem to be shaken by sufferings. Therefore, they could be indented in the diagram, to show their subordination to the main affirmations. Alternatively they could be appropriately labeled, perhaps with the symbol A" in the left margin, and those that are basic affirmations in the flow of the argument with the symbol A'.

How does all this affect our paragraph outline and our message? It would seem that we ought to alter it somewhat, perhaps as follows:

The results of our justification are—
1. Peace (v. 1)
2. Hope
   A. Hope of God's glory (v. 2)
   B. Hope even in suffering (vv. 3–4)
   C. Hope because of God's love shown in the cross (vv. 5–10)
3. Joy (v. 11)

That last point could also have been expressed as follows:

3. Joy
   A. In hope (v. 2)
   B. In sufferings (v. 3)
   C. In God Himself (v. 11)

Such a modification involves two problems. First, it alters the order in which the topics appear in the text. This, however, is a case where the inspired *pattern* may be more useful sermonically than the inspired *order*. Second, there is some repetition if we also keep the subheadings of hope as presently listed under point 2. I find no more problem with this than when looking at a tapestry that has a number of intersecting patterns. One does not detract from the beauty of the tapestry by following these patterns. In fact, it would take away from its beauty if we were to select only one and follow it across in isolation from the others. To repeat some points that occur both sequentially and in some cross-pattern will not negate the text; it will reinforce it.

I have introduced these matters at this point not to complicate the structuring of a paragraph outline, but because the complications are indeed there. It is relatively easy to find a few ideal examples to present in an exegesis, hermeneutics, or homiletics class, or to use in a book like this. But the preacher will find few "textbook" examples. The moment we begin to make such an outline, we are faced with variations. There is no point in frustrating the reader by making it seem more easy than it is. From the very beginning we need to be asking not only, what are the main and the subordinate clauses, but what is the sequence of ideas? What are the main affirmations? What modifies, explains, supports (and so on) these affirmations? Also, we must keep in mind that even when an outline is finally formed, it is still only that, an outline. It is not yet a sermon.

Inductive Outline

There is another method of analyzing a passage that I have found especially helpful in outlining sermons. It consists of three parts (see illustration below). The first part entered is a series of horizontal boxes representing the major verse divisions of the paragraph. (This system can also be used to list the major sections of a larger unit, even an entire book.) The divisions are determined by the actual thought units of the passage, apart from any homiletical considerations. The verse numbers are written in each box. Slanted lines are then drawn, from the boxes upward and to the right. On these lines one writes a brief phrase that objectively describes the contents of the small section. The reason for doing this is to establish the actual content of each section as a means of control over our interpretive and homiletical ideas.

The next step is to group these small sections in larger units that might be used as units in a sermon. By drawing a number of horizontal lines and vertical dividers below the row of boxes, I can provide for a number of tentative section titles that might be used as topics and subtopics in my sermon. I can experiment as much as I want, simply adding more lines as needed. There are several advantages to this method: (1) It fosters integrity in the analysis of the text. I can compare my proposed outline headings directly with the content titles immediately above. (2) This method forces the exegetically minded preacher to think in terms of topics, and the topically minded preacher to keep close to the passage. (3) It is a help in developing themes coherently. (4) It encourages flexibility, because it is easy to sketch out a number of different topical combinations. (5) It provides a worksheet that can be extended as far as desired, and which permits easy review, changes, and a visual basis for final decision. Writing out several separate outlines on successive sheets of paper fails to provide such advantages. For more examples, one can consult books that use this method in inductive Bible study. See especially the book by Irving L. Jenson.[14]

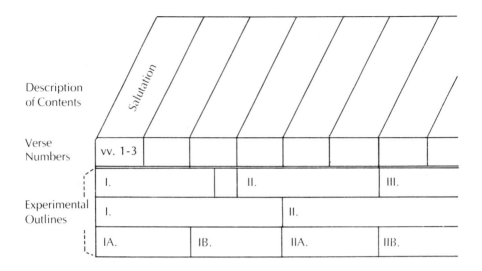

Description
of Contents

Salutation

Verse
Numbers

vv. 1-3

Experimental
Outlines

I.   II.   III.

I.   II.

IA.   IB.   IIA.   IIB.

Chapter Four

The Facts: Narrative and Compositional Patterns

We have seen that even where there is a clear sequence of thought, indicated principally by a succession of clauses, there may be cross patterns that contribute to the structure and meaning. Romans 5:1–11, which had a very clear clause structure, also had a pattern of "equivalents." Such patterns, and other types we shall consider, serve three purposes. (1) They draw the attention of the reader (especially of the Greek text) to conceptual relationships he or she might not otherwise have observed. (2) They can provide a structure for a sermon outline. (3) They contribute to the stylistic excellence of the work. We shall be concerned only with the first two aspects.

Narrative Patterns

Various cultures have differing ways of relating stories. This is too technical a matter for us here, but we do need to be aware that there are certain conventions that are followed in narration. We shall look at just a few examples where patterns can help us to understand and to preach from a narrative passage.

Specialists in Bible translation are aware of the importance of discourse analysis. An excellent example appeared in the *Bible Translator* outlining the narrative pattern found in Luke 9:57–62.[15] In this story, Jesus converses with three people in succession about the cost of discipleship. The basic pattern is already clear to the reader. Although there is no character delineation as such, except as can be deduced from the conversation, the story revolves around the three characters. The inner pattern, however, involves not the persons but the conversations. In the first conversation, it is the inquirer who takes initiative: "I will follow you wherever you go." Jesus' reply cautions the would-be disciple that the Son of Man had no place to lay his head (implying that his disciples had none either). In the second conversation, it is Jesus who initiates the conversation, saying, "Follow me." This time the visitor raises the objection, saying he needed to return home until such time as his father was laid to rest. In the third conversation, the inquirer takes both roles. He initiates the conversation about discipleship and also raises the objection.

Looking at the narrative again, we see that in the first and last instance the conversation has two sides, that is, a man speaks and Jesus speaks. This is true even though in the last conversation the man has already expressed both desire and objection, as Jesus adds a comment. In the middle conversation, however, there are three phases to the dialogue, within which Jesus mentions the kingdom of God. Proclamation of the kingdom is thus underlined as the mission of the disciple.

In addition to that, the third conversation ends with a reference to the kingdom of God. In this way, the kingdom receives emphasis in two crucial places, at the center and at the end of the narrative. Not only that, in each place the words, "kingdom of God" occur at the end of the sentence. In the central spot, the issue is the task of the disciple: proclamation of the kingdom. In the final spot the issue is the fate of any would-be disciple who fails to follow through: exclusion from kingdom service.

We could also observe that the entire narrative is introduced by the words, "As they were walking along the road." This portrays Jesus and his disciples carrying out the mission of going from place to place with the news of the kingdom. In this particular location in Luke it also portrays Jesus' progress toward Jerusalem, his city of destiny, which is a major theme in Luke. This deliberate orientation towards Jerusalem began a few verses earlier in 9:51.

The expositor will want to take all this into account as he prepares the passage for preaching. The patterns are part of the inspired text. They help us understand the dynamics of the conversation and the theological and personal issues. Obviously the patterns also launch our sermon outline.

The patterns involved in this passage are of several types. We saw that there were three characters, although there was no development of personal characteristics other than reluctance to serve for various reasons. There was also a pattern of repetition, as the circumstance of a dialogue about discipleship occurred three times.

The narrative was so simple and straightforward that there was no inner movement as such, but there was an inner pattern of conversation and also of ideas. Further, the ideological pattern was very strongly featured by means of centralizing one statement about the kingdom and of reserving the other for a climax by end stress. While few narratives in the Gospels or Acts are so neat in structure, the patterns observed here are found in other passages as well.

One of the best known parables, the Prodigal Son, is a magnificent illustration of intertwining patterns. This is seen in the very fact that this is sometimes preached as a parable not only about the Prodigal Son, but about the Waiting Father, to use Thielicke's famous and happy phrase, and also about the Elder Brother. Just as in an optical illusion the various planes and lines can be seen as leading to one perspective and then another, so the elements in this story can be viewed as directing attention to the son, to the father, or to the elder brother.

Contemporary structuralism also offers some insights as to the analysis of the parable.[16] Structuralism, in its literary dimension, is an approach that seeks to determine how literature fits into commonly observed structures not only of narrative, but also of human values and behavior across cultures and periods of history. The son can certainly be seen as the *subject,* but, in structuralist language, he is also the *receiver* of the actions of the father, who is the *sender.* The elder brother is clearly the *opponent.* The foregoing is a very simplified description of what structuralists call an *actantial* analysis (an approach now subject to considerable debate). In addition to this dimension, we need to see what *functions* characterize the narrative sequence. There are a number of functions that have been observed in structural studies, two of which are clearly observable here. They are separation and union, and loss and gain. (Different scholars will use different terminologies.)

In addition to the traditional concentration on characters and events, and to the contemporary insights of structuralism, there are observations that remain for the expositor to discover for himself in the text. The relations between the two sons and their father are graphically contrasted in the use of personal pronouns. In verse 24, the father calls the prodigal "this son of mine." In verse 27 a servant identifies the prodigal to the older brother as "your brother." But when the older brother speaks about the prodigal to the father (v. 30), he does not call him "my brother," but "this son of yours," thereby indicating his hostility and sense of estrangement from him. However, the father speaks warmly to the elder brother, calling him "my son" (v. 31), and then brings the whole story to a climax by means of the significant expression, "this brother of yours" (v. 32). That attempt to rejoin the elder brother with the prodigal illustrates the issue that underlies the parable: the Pharisees refused to welcome the sinners who, through Jesus' ministry, were returning to God (v. 1–2).

There is much more that could be introduced here as to the study of the parable, but this will serve to show how the expositor can gain from careful observation of narrative patterns. He needs to ask questions about the literary dynamics as well as about such obvious things as characters and events. The expositor will need to identify with the people, situations, and feelings of the parable. To think in terms of gain and loss, separation and reunion, will help him to enter into the overarching structure of human experience as well as the individual story. Since his own congregation is experiencing separation and reunion, loss and gain, and since in contemporary life, just as in first-century stories, there are senders and receivers, helpers and opponents, awareness of these structural patterns is a *sine qua non* for the expositor who would also be a pastor. If earlier expositors lacked structuralist insights and terminology, the more successful ones certainly had an intuitive awareness that helped them.

Compositional Patterns

These are patterns that lie more on the surface of the passage. They may occur in a narrative or in a logical argument. Some are marked by specific words or constructions (e.g., a subordinating conjunction that indicates causality or, at the other extreme, a gradual progression of ideas or events). Often these compositional patterns are marked by semantic patterns, which we will discuss in the next chapter. It will be useful to consult both chapters together when preparing sermons so as to be alert to both kinds of patterns at once. This approach is familiar to those who are interested in inductive methods of Bible study. There are two books which I have found especially helpful with respect to this kind of pattern. One is *Methodical Bible Study* by Robert A. Traina.[17] The other is *Independent Bible Study* by Irving Jenson.[18] The logical or compositional patterns they describe are used in the study of the English Bible, but are equally applicable to the study of the Greek text. They are certainly valuable in the determination of both the content of a passage and the form of the sermon. There are twelve kinds of patterns that I believe can be very useful to the expositor.

Comparison or Contrast

This pattern is obvious in Romans 5:12–19, where Adam and Christ are contrasted in an alternating pattern. In Luke 7:36–50 there is a contrast between Simon the Pharisee and the sinful woman, especially in verses 44–47. Although this pattern does not provide the structure for the whole passage, as is the case in Romans 5:12–19, it does form the basis for the declaration of verse 47. Romans 4:1–25 teaches justification by faith through the example of Abraham. This is easily seen as a comparison between Abraham's justification and ours. Whatever the clause structure may be in such passages, the logical way to structure a sermon is according to the points of comparison. An exception would be Luke 7, where the contrasts in verses 44–45 are an inner, less important motif, which serves to heighten the basic contrast between the two people and their attitudes toward sin and forgiveness.

Romans 8 provides a further example of contrasts. Paul contrasts setting the mind on the things of the Spirit with setting the mind on the things of the flesh. Present sufferings with future glory are also set in contrast. Galatians 5 has the familiar contrast between the works of the flesh and the fruit of the Spirit. Ephesians 5 contrasts light and darkness, drunkenness with wine and the filling of the Spirit. New Testament passages and New Testament theology are full of contrasts. Christianity itself demands a choice between two contrasting "ways," between life and death.

Repetition

This compositional device is a simple one, sometimes reflecting a Semitic style. A well-known example is the Beatitudes in the Sermon on the Mount (Matthew 5:3–11). If this kind of repetition becomes the basis for points of a sermon, great care needs to be taken lest it be tedious or trite. Some questions will need to be addressed, for example, "Who is the person God blesses?" In verses 21–48 of the same chapter Matthew presents Jesus' series of "antitheses." In this series Jesus places his own teaching against that which the people had heard. Each section begins with the words, "you have heard. . . ." This occurs five times. To pick up one more example from Matthew, in chapter 23 there is a series of woes pronounced by Jesus on the Pharisees. For an example outside of the Gospels we can go to Ephesians 4. "There is one body and one spirit . . . one hope . . . one Lord . . . one faith . . . one baptism . . . one God . . ." (vv. 4–6). Whether or not the various elements in such a series are suitable for transformation into successive points of a sermon, the sermon must, if it is to be faithful to the text, draw attention to the series. It is there to draw attention both to the individual items and to their cumulative effect. This is a literary device used under the inspiration of the Holy Spirit, and should be allowed to have its full impact.

Continuity

Here we refer to passages that may or may not have a repeated word or phrase, but do have a common theme. Matthew 13:24–52 contains the well-known series of kingdom parables. In this case there is a repetition of the phrase "the kingdom of heaven is like . . . ," but there are other teachings on and through the parables that occur before and even during this series. Before the series we have the parable of the Sower and Jesus' comments on why he speaks in parables. Within the series is a quotation from Psalm 78:2 about parables. While the expositor may find it advisable to treat the parables and other comments individually, he should not treat them independently. There is a cumulative effect that must be captured if we are to grasp the full import of what Jesus is teaching about the kingdom and those who enter it.

In Matthew 4:1–11 and Luke 4:1–12 we have the account of Jesus' temptation in the desert. Even though each temptation is unique, none can be isolated from the others or the significance of the passage is lessened. We shall return to these passages in a moment. Luke 5:17–6:11 contains a series of different incidents in the life of Jesus. Yet, here too there is a continuity marked by a reference in each situation to the Pharisees. Taken together they illustrate the characteristics of Jesus and of his ministry that the Pharisees criticized. This series occurs in basically the same form in Mark and, in different locations in Matthew. However, there is an element of continuity in Luke that is lacking in Matthew and Mark. Luke mentions the Pharisees in each incident. In addition to that, he mentions the Pharisees at the very beginning of the first incident, the healing of the paralytic. Neither Matthew nor Mark even mention the Pharisees, and only introduce the scribes in the middle of the story. Luke is the only writer who mentions the Pharisees in the final incident, the healing of the man with the shriveled hand (Luke 6:6–11). Therefore, we realize that although Mark sees a continuity here with respect to a series of controversial actions by Jesus and his disciples, Luke shows us even more: there is a hostile group of observers, the Pharisees. Luke will go on to show that the "people" are open to Jesus' teaching, but the Pharisees, as a whole, are not. This is part of Luke's design to show that Christianity grows out of Judaism and was recognized as a legitimate religion by the Jewish people. It is not the people but their leaders who were bent on rejecting Jesus.

I have chosen examples of continuity from the Gospels because this is less obvious in the Gospels than in the Epistles. We tend to fragment the various incidents and teachings in the Gospels, failing to observe their interrelationship, and therefore failing to preach them properly. If we were to select passages from the Epistles as examples of continuity, our thoughts would probably turn first to the series of gifts in Romans 12 and 1 Corinthians 12.

Climax

We referred above to the narrative about Jesus' temptation in Matthew 4 and Luke 4. There are three temptations, different in nature but with much in common. Not only so, but the evangelists present the second and third temptations in a different order. This is not a problem with regard to historicity, but it is a phenomenon that deserves the attention of the biblical interpreter and preacher. Although certainty is not possible, it seems very probable that Matthew has been led by the Spirit of God to put the temptation regarding the kingdoms of the world in the last place for the sake of reaching a climax appropriate to the royal messianic theme in Matthew's gospel. Luke, on the other hand, emphasizes the Jewish origins of Christianity and is constantly, both in the gospel and in Acts, using Jerusalem and the temple in particular as symbolic of this relationship. Consequently, it would seem most appropriate for him to have the final incident which takes place at the temple in Jerusalem, in last place. If this is true, it illustrates the importance of observing where the climax of an event or series of statements occurs. This is usually in the last place of a series.

Whether or not our interpretation of the order of the temptations is correct, the literary function of climax is important enough to make this kind of inquiry whenever there is a series of any form. The account in Matthew 8:5–13 and that in Luke 7:1–10 about the centurion's servant differ from each other in certain ways appropriate to each gospel. Both accounts, however, conclude with a statement that the servant was healed. In Matthew the statement is made at the moment Jesus made his pronouncement. In Luke they find the servant healed when they return. In each case the healing forms the climax to the story, even though the declaration occurs at different points chronologically. We shall return to this story for another observation shortly.

In the familiar story of Jesus sleeping in the boat during a storm, the climax is not, as so often preached, in the calming of the wind and waves. It is rather the disciples' question at the end of the story: "Who is this? He commands even the winds and the water, and they obey him" (Luke 8:25; cf. Matthew 8:27; Mark 4:41). In Luke this question has an important place as the first of the three questions about Jesus' identity observed above (cf. Luke 9:9, where Herod asks, "Who, then, is this?" and Luke 9:20, Jesus' question, "Who do you say I am?"). To preach only the application that Jesus quiets the storms of our lives is to miss the more important lesson, the true identity of the one who performed the miracle.

The climax to the Transfiguration narrative is, in each gospel that records it, the voice from the cloud. This focuses attention on God's declaration concerning his Son. Final emphasis in the narrative is thereby placed not on what was observed, not even the transfiguration of Christ, but on God's explicit declaration concerning the meaning of that transfiguration. Interestingly, Peter's reference to the Transfiguration in 2 Peter 1:16–18 also emphasizes the words from heaven. He then goes on to speak of the word of the prophets in verses 19–21. A message on the Transfiguration should therefore also find its climax in the proclamation of God's declaration concerning his dear Son.

We referred earlier to the "controversy stories" in Luke 5:17–6:11 and the parallels in Matthew and Mark. It is appropriate now to observe that in each gospel the series of incidents ends with a statement that the leaders plotted to do away with Jesus.

Therefore, a sermon that concentrates exclusively on, for example, Jesus teaching about the Sabbath misses the function of the stories in the Gospel narrative.

In Ephesians chapter 4 the repetition of the word "one," which we observed earlier, has a double climax. The final statement in verse 6, "one God and Father of all who is over all and through all and in all," climaxes the confession of faith. However, the word "one" occurs one more time for a different kind of climax. Verse 7 begins with that final occurrence that, in the Greek text is in the dative case, "to each one." The reader of the Greek is probably more likely to catch that than the reader of the English. The point is that after using the word "one" in a series to refer to unity, Paul now uses the same word, "one," to refer to individuality. In this way, Paul introduces the truth of our individuality both as a climax to the series of references to our unity and as an introduction to the section on the individual gifts God has given to his church (vv. 7–13).

A different kind of double climax is found at the end of Romans chapter 7. In 6:16–8:8, Paul is dealing largely with the validity and function of God's law. The series of four rhetorical questions in chapters 6 and 7 concludes with "Did that which is good, then, become death to me?" (7:13). He addresses this final question both from theology and from personal experience. The climax to his personal experience is expressed first in verses 24–25 in terms of wretchedness and deliverance. The climax to his theological argument follows this in verse 25. He then goes on to discuss the consequence of all this in chapter 8.

Paul's discussion of God's ways with Israel in chapters 9–11 reaches its climax in the majestic doxology of 11:33–36, "Oh, the depth of the riches of the wisdom and knowledge of God! . . . To Him be the glory forever! Amen." Another doxology climaxes Paul's prayer in Ephesians 3:14–21. The idea of a doxological climax appears frequently in the Gospel of Luke and in Acts. Such is the case when people observe the work of God, as for example, in a healing by the Lord Jesus. One instance of this, which occurs in all three synoptic Gospels, is the climax of the healing of the paralytic who was let down through the roof. Those who saw this "glorified God" (or "praised God," Matthew 9:8; Mark 2:12; Luke 5:26). Luke also mentions that the former paralytic went home, "praising God" (Luke 5:26). In our concern to teach doctrine and to make practical applications in our sermons, we must be careful not to overlook this most important of all goals, the worship of God. How many of our sermons truly reach this climax?

Cruciality

This refers either to a point in a narrative or logical argument that is of extreme importance, or to a significant turning point. The story about the healing of the centurion's servant reached its climax, as we saw, in the concluding statement that the healing was accomplished. However, there is an earlier point in the story that is crucial both in the narrative itself and in its significance for us. That is the expression of the centurion's faith and its commendation by Jesus. Without this the story could not have proceeded. Without it the story would probably not have been included in Scripture. The expression of that faith by a Gentile is what gives the story its particular meaning. The expression and commendation of that faith is the turning point in the narrative. It should also have this place in the sermon. If our attempt to structure the sermon into evenly portioned parts diminishes the particular importance of this turning point in the minds of the congregation, our sermon structure will have distorted the meaning of the passage. To be faithful to the meaning of Scripture in this case means to draw attention to this crucial point.

If we were to discuss examples of cruciality in the New Testament, one would probably come to mind immediately. That is the confession of Peter, "You are the Christ, the Son of the living God" (Matthew 16:16 and parallels). This is the crucial point not only of the passage, but of each of the synoptic Gospels and indeed of the entire ministry of the Lord Jesus.

Another example may not be as easily recognized. In Revelation 10, following the sounding of the "seventh trumpet" an angel makes a solemn pronouncement "by him who lives forever and ever, who created the heavens and all that is in them, the earth and all that is in it, and the sea and all that is in it." The very wording of this awesome oath alerts us as to the importance of what is to be said. The next words are "there will be no more delay!" Earlier in Revelation the martyrs cried out "How long, Sovereign Lord, holy and true, until you judge the inhabitants of the earth and avenge our blood?" (6:10). The question, "How long?" stands along side that other question so frequently asked, "Why?" We grapple with the "problem of evil" and the "mystery of iniquity" (2 Thessalonians 2:7). Meanwhile, stage by stage and age by age God is revealing his "mystery," his purpose and plan that he is working out through earth's history. Now, here in Revelation 10, "delay" has ended and "the mystery of God will be accomplished, just as he announced to his servants the prophets" (v. 7). Clearly this is a crucial point in the Book of Revelation, in the experience of God's people, and in the history of the world. The cruciality of the moment is further proclaimed in the words "The kingdom of the world has become the kingdom of our Lord and of his Christ, and he will reign forever and ever" (11:15).

Interchange

This feature was observed above when we noted the alternation of persons as the subject of Luke's narrative in chapters 1 and 2. Luke draws our attention first to the approaching birth of John the Baptist, then to that of Jesus, and then turns to one and the other alternately. Another example is the interchange involving Jairus's daughter and the woman with hemorrhage (Mark 5:21–43 and parallels). In Romans 5:12–19 there is an alternation (as well as basic contrast) between Adam and Christ. Romans 7:7–25 presents an interchange between the law and the human recognition of its validity on the one hand and the law of sin and death with our fleshly sin and failure on the other. Paul moves back and forth from the one to the other as the argument proceeds.

Particularization

Matthew 6 continues Jesus' Sermon on the Mount with the words, "be careful not to do your 'acts of righteousness' before men to be seen by them." Jesus then moves from this generalization about "acts of righteousness" to a particularization. He deals specifically with alms given to the needy (v. 2), prayer (v. 5), and fasting (v. 16).

Matthew and Luke both describe the ministry of John the Baptist. John tells those who gathered to hear him to produce fruit in keeping with repentance (Matthew 3:8; Luke 3:8). Only Luke particularizes this general exhortation. In verses 10–14, in response to the question of the crowds, "What should we do then?" Luke talks of sharing clothing, of responsibility in tax collecting, and of self-restraint on the part of soldiers. The passage in Ephesians 4 that we cited earlier as an example of climax, could also be given as an example of particularization. After speaking of the unity of the body in verses 3–6, where Paul repeats the word "one" he goes on to speak of our individuality, "But to each one of us grace has been given . . ." (v. 7). Following this Paul specifies the gifts God has given to his church in verses 11–13. Likewise in Romans 12 and 1 Corinthians 12 Paul particularizes God's gifts.

This literary device of particularization is of special help to the preacher because it is our responsibility to take the biblical truths about God and his world and apply them in particular ways to our own situation. Particularization leads to application.

Generalization.

This, of course, is the reverse of particularization. Beginning again with the Sermon on the Mount, we read in Matthew 5:21–47 of a number of specific examples of the moral standard Jesus sets for his followers. At the conclusion of these particular examples of adultery, oaths, etc., Jesus concludes with the generalization, "Be perfect, therefore, as your heavenly Father is perfect." He states another generalization in 7:12: "In everything, do to others what you would have them do to you, for this sums up the Law and the Prophets." Although this follows several verses of teaching on prayer, it functions as a generalization that summarizes the basic thrust of the Sermon on the Mount. It is followed by the injunction, "Enter through the narrow gate . . ." and the warning against false prophets and false profession. The sermon concludes with the parable of the house on the rock and the statement that Jesus "taught as one who had authority" (7:29).

For an example from the Epistles we may turn to Romans 13. There Paul lists some of the duties of a responsible Christian citizen (vv. 6–7). He follows this particularization with a generalization: "Let no debt remain outstanding except the continuing debt to love one another" (v. 8). The preacher who recognizes this as a generalization that relates back to the particulars in verses 6 and 7 will not make the mistake of exhorting his congregation against going into financial debt on the basis of verse 8! Generalization helps us to find a principle for living.

Cause to Effect

For an example from the Gospels, we may look at Matthew 21:33–46. The Parable of the Tenants with its teaching on the rejection of

Jesus by those who should have honored him is clearly the cause of the attempt of the leaders to arrest him (vv. 45 and 46). The same effect receives even greater attention in the Gospel of John, this time as a result of the raising of Lazarus. After that miracle and the response of many Jews who then believed in Jesus (11:45), the leaders decide that the time has come to put Jesus out of the way (vv. 47–53). This also provides another example of "Cruciality." This is clearly a turning point in Jesus' life. Chapter 11 concludes with orders being given to report Jesus' whereabouts so that he could be arrested (v. 57). John's Passion narrative begins immediately with the very next verse (12:1). Passover is at hand, and Mary anoints Jesus for "the day of [his] burial" (v. 7).

Romans 1:18–32 provides a good example of "Cause to Effect." Here Paul lists the shameful sins of humankind. In verse 32 we learn that the ultimate effect of such sin is death, but the immediate effect of perversion is continuance and even approval among those who do this.

Sometimes the distinction between effect and purpose is unclear. This is partly due to our occasional uncertainty as to whether to interpret the Greek particle ἵνα as "in order that" (purpose) or "so that" (result). Often, considering the providence of God, the distinction is not important. If an effect is clearly intended, we may consider it as a statement of purpose. For example, in 1 Corinthians 2:1–5, Paul explains why he did not preach with eloquence. The reason, which is also the effect of his action, is "so that your faith might not rest on men's wisdom, but on God's power." This parallels the preceding paragraph, in which Paul explains that God did not choose many talented people, "so that no one may boast before him" (1:29) and so that we will boast only "in the Lord" (v. 31).

It is particularly important that the preacher observe cause and effect (along with purpose), because it is the preacher's business to make people aware of the import of their own actions and decisions. In a sense, the entire Bible is a series of cause and effect relationships. This is perhaps most clear in the Old Testament prophets. It is important to scrutinize passages looking for this kind of relationship, because it is sometimes implied rather than overtly stated. Whether covert or part of a clear compositional pattern, the message, if present, should have the same force in the sermon that it has in the text.

Substantiation

This means providing the grounds for reason for something. For example, in Matthew 16:24-27 Jesus speaks of taking up the cross and gaining true life. The importance of the issues involved becomes clear in verse 27: "For the Son of Man . . . will reward each person according to what he has done." If we preach on discipleship from this passage, but fail to provide the substantiation that Jesus himself does, we have failed to give Jesus' teaching in perspective and in its fullness.

Jesus' teaching about possessions in Luke 12:13–34 receives its substantiation in several stages. For example verse 31 assures us that to those who seek God's kingdom "these things will be given to you as well" (v. 31). At the end of the next paragraph (vv. 32–34), which includes the word "treasure," Jesus words his substantiation as follows: "For where your treasure is, there your heart will be also." If we exhort our congregation to take costly action, we fail them and do not do justice to our Lord's teachings if we do not provide the basis for assurance he has given with regard to such action. Our exhortation may turn out to be pleading, threatening, or cajoling, with anything but a proper motivation, if we miss the motivation given in the biblical text. This substantiation can occur in many types of biblical teaching. In the examples above it is a basis for obedience. It may also be a basis for biblical doctrines or divine promises. We often quote Romans 8:28. But do we go on to provide the substantiation for the affirmation that God works for our good in all things? That promise has often seemed hollow to people who have experienced tragedy in their lives. The substantiation comes in verses 29 and 30. Here we see God's sovereignty and purpose. Verse 29 begins "For . . . ," which translates the Greek ὅτι, which is often translated "because." The reason we "know" that God is working for our good is explained in verses 29 and 30, which conclude "those he justified, he also glorified."

Other examples abound in the Epistles. The familiar verses, "For it is by grace you have been saved . . ." (Ephesians 2:8ff.) are themselves a substantiation for the teaching Paul has been giving in that chapter. The next chapter in Ephesians begins, "For this reason . . ." (3:1). In this case it is what has preceded that provides the substantiation for what he is about to say (ultimately his prayer in vv. 14–21).

To continue in Ephesians, we may note that Paul's warnings against immorality in 5:3–7 are not empty words but are based on two solemn facts. (1) "For of this you can be sure: No immoral, impure or greedy person . . . has any inheritance in the kingdom of Christ and of God," and (2) ". . . for because of such things God's wrath comes on those who are disobedient" (vv. 5–6).

If we as preachers are concerned to persuade and motivate people to make crucial decisions in their lives for God, we must provide a biblical motivation for this. If we are going to persuade people to acknowledge the truths God presents in his Word, we must provide an adequate logical basis for such acceptance. Once again, if we attempt to do this by our own powers of persuasion, neglecting the very substantiation that God provides in his own words, we have substituted the weak arm of the flesh for the power of God's Spirit speaking through his inspired Word.

Radiation

Of all the compositional patterns discussed so far, this one probably offers the least structural help for a sermon outline. Recognition of the pattern will, nevertheless, alert us to the type and amount of material that should be considered together. In radiation there is a central theme that radiates outward in various directions. The idea is developed first in one way and then in another. Mark 7 and Matthew 23 contain a number of comments Jesus made about the Pharisees. Some progression is found in Mark 7, which we shall observe shortly, and Matthew 23 features the repetition of the word "woe," as we observed above. Apart from this it is difficult to find a clear logical structure.

Chapters 12 and 16 of Luke record various teachings of the Lord Jesus on the subject of material possessions. There are clear interrelationships, but not in linear order. In 1 Corinthians 15 there is a succession of comments on the subject of the Resurrection. The points Paul is making here follow one another naturally, but are more logically connected with the basic theme than they are with each other. This, however, does not preclude building a logical sermon outline on the passage.

Progression

It is not always easy to tell when an author is consciously establishing a progression of thought. Because John tends to use synonyms with little differentiation in meaning, it is hard to know whether the succession of different Greek words for "see" in the Resurrection narrative of John 20:3–9 is intended to signify a growth in perception.

The progression in Mark 7 is more clear. In verse 8 Jesus says, "You have let go (ἀφέντες) of the commands of God and are holding on to the traditions of men." In verse 9 he says, "You have a fine way of setting aside (ἀθετεῖτε) the commands of God . . . ." Jesus concludes in verse 13: "Thus you nullify (ἀκυροῦντες) the word of God by your tradition . . . ." This also embodies the literary feature of equivalents. Each statement has a reference to the commands or Word of God and to the tradition of the Pharisees, but the verb is different in each case ("let go," "setting aside," "nullify"). The element of progression lies in the fact that each of these is progressively more serious an offense against God's commandments.

Romans 1:18–32 contains a progression. In this case the central activities of humankind seem to degenerate further and further as the chapter continues. Ephesians 4:11–13 is probably to be understood as a progression also. God gives gifted leaders; they prepare God's people; God's people do works of service; the body of Christ is built up; we all reach unity in the faith and in the knowledge of the Son of God; we become mature, finally "attaining to the whole measure of the fullness of Christ." Another progression occurs later in the same chapter. If a robber is converted, he should (1) "steal no longer," (2) "work," (3) "share with those in need" (v. 28).

It is already apparent that when we discipline ourselves to be alert for these twelve compositional patterns we accomplish two things. First, we are likely to find a pattern that itself can form the basis for a sermon outline. Second, and more important, we will tend to follow closely the author's own direction of thought, rather than to superimpose our own impressions.

Chapter Five

The Facts:
Semantic Patterns

The Importance of Semantic Patterns

Semantic patterns may be formed by parts of words (morphemes), words, or even whole phrases. There are simple patterns that are signalled by similar sounds or appearance in the Greek. But there are other patterns that involve various relationships of meaning. To trace these requires careful observation and lexical study. It also requires mature judgment so as to determine accurately which patterns are truly significant and which are merely stylistic or even unintentional. Semantic patterns are generally less helpful in structuring a sermon than are narrative or compositional patterns. However they can be surprisingly helpful in two ways. First, they may alert the reader to the larger compositional patterns. A few words which stand in contrast to each other, for example, can signal a major compositional framework of contrast. Second, semantic patterns may reveal a number of ideas that do not surface into the main outline of an author's thought. They are like the small brush strokes that apply harmonizing or contrasting colors to give a painting further definition and beauty. The expositor who is bent on framing his sermonic house (to change the metaphor) using the more obvious pieces of lumber from the text, may miss those supportive and decorative pieces that turn a structure into a livable and unique home. Writers of the New Testament do not use literary devices for aesthetic effect alone; they use them for spiritual effect. They even use them, at times, as part of the basic framing.

We find a beautiful example of both functions, basic material for an outline and supplementary material for spiritual effect, in Hebrews 1:1–4. The epistle opens with two words of such similar sound that the effect could not possibly have missed those who heard it read: πολυμερῶς καὶ πολυτρόπως. These words, meaning "at many times and in various ways," serve to introduce the message of Hebrews about God's final revelation in Christ by drawing attention to the fragmentary nature of the Old Testament revelation. The scattered way in which God spoke over a period of time, in many circumstances, and through many different people is in stark contrast to the focus of God's revelation through the person of his Son in first-century Palestine. This is not only a precise logical introduction to the argument of this book, but it is a superb attention getter. The similarity of sound makes the reader or hearer sit up and take notice of what is being said. It is the kind of rhetorical device that is not ultimately for an aesthetic effect but for a spiritual one.

The author of Hebrews continues with a series of contrasts. This is the kind of compositional patterns we just observed above. In this case it involves certain semantic patterns. There are a series of words and phrases that, while not technically antonyms or polar opposites, function as such in this context. These include: (1) πάλαι ("long-ago," "in ancient times," or NIV: "in the past") in contrast to ἐπ᾽ ἐσχάτου τῶν ἡμερῶν τούτων ("in the last of these days," or "in these last days"); (2) τοῖς πατράσιν ("to our fathers," or NIV: "to our forefathers") in contrast to ἡμῖν ("to us"); (3) ἐν τοῖς προφήταις ("through the prophets") in contrast to ἐν υἱῷ ("by his Son"). The author has heightened the contrast even further by setting this series of opposites into two types of clauses. The references to the Old Testament revelation are set in a participial dependent clause (λαλήσας. . . , "having spoken"), whereas the description of God's final revelation in Christ is set in the main clause with the verb in the aorist indicative (ἐλάλησεν, "he spoke").

At the conclusion of this paragraph in Hebrews 1, the author desires to show the superiority of Christ over the angels. He does this by comparing the "name" of the angels to the far superior name of the Son. Most translations, especially those that attempt to be literal like the NASB, stumble over this verse, producing a rather awkward translation. The NIV cuts through the fog of misunderstanding by recognizing that two different words in the Greek text are best translated as synonyms, because, although they have slight lexical differences, their meanings do overlap. Their function here is to facilitate a comparison. Rather than translating κρείττων as "better" and διαφορώτερον as "excellent," as in the NASB: "having become as much better than the angels, as He has inherited a more excellent name than they," the NIV translates both words "superior." This results in the very simple and clear comparison: "So he became as much superior to the angels as the name he has inherited is superior to theirs." In this way, the recognition of a semantic pattern has resulted in a better translation and, importantly for us, also in a better sermonic structure. With these clear patterns at both the beginning and the end of this opening paragraph, the preacher can structure a sermon that is both well ordered and faithful to the intent of the passage. This also means that he will have a clear understanding as to the direction that the author of Hebrews is taking in the succeeding paragraphs as he utilizes a series of contrasts to show the superiority of the Son of God.

We shall not go into this much detail for each semantic pattern. This example should alert us to the possibilities of discovery. The following categories are briefly noted to alert us to the kinds of patterns that may be fruitful for our study and sermon preparation.

Categories of Semantic Patterns

Synonyms

Most preachers, especially those of an earlier generation, have probably heard of the work written over one hundred years ago by Richard Chenevix Trench, *Synonyms of the New Testament*.[19] Contemporary students know that his analysis of various Greek synonyms needs to be revised in the light of more recent lexical studies. Nevertheless it stands not only as a helpful work but as a monument to the richness of the Greek vocabulary. Our interest here, however, is not so much with those synonyms that are scattered throughout the New Testament, but with words of fairly similar meaning that occur in proximity within a passage or its context. We have already seen that classification of synonyms is not an easy matter. In John 20, the author uses three different words to indicate the act of seeing; βλέπει (v. 5), θεωρεῖ (v. 6), and εἶδεν (v. 8). Although some have suggested that these represent an increase in perception, that is hard to substantiate from the words themselves. However, even if the words are sufficiently interchangeable so that they cannot support by themselves an interpretation of increasing perception, John's addition of the verb "believed" shows that their perception did lead to faith.

We face a similar situation in the following chapter of John with the familiar interchange of the verbs ἀγάπαω and φιλέω ("love"). Many preachers have distinguished these two words, and it is true that in this case, as with the verbs for seeing just discussed, that there are shades of meaning between them. However, once again it is difficult to assert confidently that John intended to convey a clear difference between them in this context. Peter's grief because Jesus asked him a third time, "Do you love me?" (v. 17) is more likely because Jesus repeated the question three times, thereby recalling Peter's three denials, than because Jesus used (in Aramaic) a different word the third time.

It is worth noting here that John not only tends to use different words synonymously but also to use one word with different meanings. The best known example of this is the use of ἄνωθεν with the double meaning of "again" and "from above" (John 3:3). It is also possible that when Jesus says, "when I am lifted up" he means not only on the cross (John 12:33) but in glory. Another example is very important for the preacher. That is John's use of the word "believe." In 2:23–25 we see that many people believed when they saw Jesus' miracles in Jerusalem, but that Jesus "would not entrust himself to them, for he knew all men." Also in John 8:30, we read that "many put their faith in him." Then Jesus speaks to those "who had believed him." His words show that they were not yet believers in the deepest truest sense. This is very clear when just a few sentences later he says that they are children of the devil. Whether or not there is a clear difference between believing Christ and believing *in* (εἰς) Christ (v. 30), the verb is the same. Also in the earlier instance in John 2:23 those whose "faith" was not to be trusted were said to have believed "in" (εἰς) his name. The expositor of the Gospel of John must work very carefully with these double meanings as well as with John's use of synonyms, if he is to be faithful to God's revelation through that Gospel in his preaching.

We find another use of synonymous terms in chapter 12 of Luke. In response to the man who asked him to make a judgment in the matter of family inheritance, Jesus said that "a man's life does not consist in the abundance of his possessions." The word for life here is ζωή (v. 15). Jesus then tells a story of the rich fool. In this story, he uses the, word ψυχή ("soul" or "life") several times, apparently as a synonym for ζωή. The word ψυχή is used again in verses 22 and 23, where the thought is fairly parallel to that of verse 15 where the other word, ζωή, is used. To be sure, these are different words, often used in different frames of reference. However, in this passage, the stress is not on their difference but on their similarity. Jesus is talking about that aspect of man that is beyond the physical or material. Here again, the NIV captures the sense of the passage better than the NASB. While the latter accurately translates ζωή as "life," and ψυχή as "soul," that distinction is really not to the point here, and results in verse 19 in the archaic, "I will say to my soul, 'Soul, ...'" The NIV begins the man's dialogue with himself with this contemporary wording: "He thought to himself, 'What shall I do?'" The words "What shall I do?" are a clever way of expressing the man's deliberation. The preacher, by using contemporary language in verse 19 (nothing theological being lost by the omission of the word "soul" in this case), and by using the word "life" for both ζωή and ψυχή, both unifies and simplifies the narrative. He thus focuses on the contrast between true life and our temporary existence in the world of the material.

Semantic Fields

Words that are not synonymous or nearly synonymous may still be related very closely. They may pertain to the same basic concept, but describe different aspects of that concept. If so they are said to be in the same semantic field. A word that belongs in a semantic field in one context can be classified in other semantic fields in other contexts if it shares certain similarities with them as well. In the example given below, I have chosen the general concept of "time." First, I have diagramed four words of somewhat contiguous meaning. The word χρόνος generally has to do with the succession of time; καιρός often signifies a particular opportune season; ὥρα not only means "hour" but also has to do, especially in John, with an appointed time; τὸ νῦν "the now," refers to one's present circumstances. A writer could use any one of these words to describe the present moment, if it were appropriate to his emphasis. They are different and yet closely related. Their relationship may be diagramed as follows.

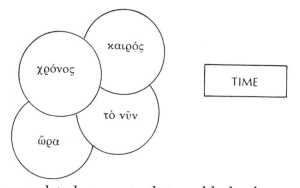

There are related concepts that could also be mentioned as belonging to the same semantic field. Specific words come to mind, such as, "age" (αἰών), "quickly," "suddenly," "the Day," to name a few. Also related are such phrases as "the coming One" (ὁ ἐρχόμενος), and Jesus' description of the place of unending torment as the place where "the worm does not die." That last phrase might seem very strange in this semantic field, and yet in Jesus' use of it he employs the idea of a continuous succession of worms or maggots, such as one would find in the Valley of Hinnom outside of Jerusalem, as a means of expressing endlessness in a repulsive and painful environment. Likewise, the words, "How long . . . until . . . ?" in Revelation 6:10, express the idea of protracted waiting under adverse circumstances, which is certainly related to the concept of time.

Awareness of semantic fields helps the preacher in two ways. It makes him sensitive to thought connections that contribute to the unity and meaning of the passage. It also causes him to think beyond individual words to dimensions of human experience. This means that we are in a better position to relate the Scriptures to the present life of our congregation. To continue the example of time, there are undoubtedly in any congregation those who are harried, hasseled by the urgent, and trying to plan well so that they can do all that they should in the time available. Some are waiting for others to act, for orders to be delivered from suppliers, for bones to heal, for children to return, or, perhaps, for spouses to be converted. Most will recall their days in the past apart from Christ, and will appreciate the time references in Ephesians 2 to "at that time" (v. 12) and "but now" (v. 13). Also all believers are waiting for the return of Christ, and even apart from details concerning the time of the rapture are stirred by thoughts of "the coming One" and the words in Hebrews 10:37, "For in just a very little while, 'He who is coming will come and will not be late.'" Likewise the words of the Lord Jesus at the conclusion of the Book of Revelation speak to our sense of time and of expectation: "Yes, I am coming soon."

Antonyms or Polar-Opposites

These, of course, are words that mean the opposite of each other. For this and the next several categories I am going to draw on Romans 5 for examples. This will help us to see the interplay of words in one passage. Romans 5:1–11 contains several antonyms. In verses 6–8, "ungodly" and "sinners" are the opposite of "righteous" and "good." In verse 10, "death" and "life" are opposites.

Overlapping Words

These are words that have distinctive meanings, but, when used in the same context, overlap to some degree in meaning. In Romans 5:9 Paul says that we have been "justified" by the "blood" of Christ. In verse 10 he says that we have been "reconciled" to God through the "death" of Christ. Paul is not here laboring the distinction between justification and reconciliation, but rather is using both terms to indicate the work that God has done to make us acceptable in his presence (cf. vv. 1–2). Likewise, although the word "blood" generally means something quite different from "death," in this context both words, "blood" and "death," refer in general to the saving work of Christ for sinners.

Contiguous Words

We observed above some contiguous words dealing with the aspect of time. In Romans 5 several words are used with reference to the state of those who have not been reconciled to God. They are "powerless," "ungodly," "sinners," and "enemies" (vv. 6–10). These words are not overlapping in meaning, but they are conceptually related.

Included

Here one word has a meaning that is included in the meaning of another word. In Romans 5:7 Paul says, "Very rarely will anyone die for a righteous man, though for a good man someone might possibly dare to die." It is difficult to know just what difference

79

Paul intends here between "righteous" and "good." One possibility is that when he speaks of a "good" man he means someone very special who is not only righteous but has in some way been someone's benefactor.[20] If this interpretation is correct, righteousness is assumed, or "included" in goodness.

Equivalents

When we discussed making a paragraph outline of Romans 5:1–11, we observed that certain phrases were similar (i.e., "equivalent") to each other, with the exception of a word or so. Note again the examples on page 53. This device enables the author to emphasize certain important words by repetition and at the same time to move his thought further by introducing new concepts at each recurrence of the phrase. In certain instances this feature can provide the structure for a sermon outline.

Cognates and Words Containing Similar Morphemes

In this category are words that may or may not be directly related to each other in their contextual meaning, but which tend to draw the reader's attention to them in tandem. Careful judgment is needed here lest we assume in a given case that the author intended to capture the reader's attention when actually it was simply a coincidental juxtaposition. We will leave Romans 5 at this point to find clear examples elsewhere. In Philippians 2:17 and 18 there is no question that Paul deliberately repeats the root χαιρ . . . (for "joy") four times. This emphasizes the idea of rejoicing and rejoicing together. In the next two verses, verses 19 and 20, he repeats the root ψυχ ("soul") and the cognates εὐψυχῶ and ἰσόψυχον. In this case the words have different meanings and one cannot categorically say whether or not Paul deliberately used them eight words apart. Yet the fact that Paul is emphasizing attitudes of heart and mind and soul in Philippians makes us ponder this similarity. It is not often recognized that the idea of mental attitude is even more prominent in Philippians than is that of joy. The word ἡγέομαι, "think" or "consider," occurs five times, in 2:3, 6, 25; 3:7–8 (twice). The word λογίζομαι, "reckon" or "consider," occurs in 3:13 and 4:8. Φρονέω is found eight times, in 1:7; 2:2 (twice), 5; 3:15, 19; 4:2, 10. The heart of the epistle is chapter 2 with its description of the "mind" (or mental attitude) of Christ. So it would be natural in 2:19–20 for Paul to point up his mental attitude of cheer (ἐυψυχῶ) and to emphasize that Timothy's concern for people showed that he had the same mental attitude (ἰσόψυχον) as Paul, by putting these similar words near each other in the text.

An unambiguous example of this device is found in Ephesians 2:5–6 and again in chapter 3:6. In the first instance he is speaking of our life, resurrection, and position with Christ in the "heavenlies." Paul uses three verbs, συνεζωοποίησεν ("made us alive with . . ."), συνήγειρεν ("raised us up with . . ."), and συνεκάθισεν ("seated us with . . ."). Obviously the repetition of the prefix συν, which means "together with," effectively ties together the three aspects of our association with the risen Christ. The example in chapter 3 involves the use of the same prefix, but this time to emphasize the unity or "togetherness" of believing Jews and Gentiles in the church. In this case the words are συγκληρονόμα, σύσσωμα, and συμμέτοχα, "heirs together," "members together," and "sharers together" (v. 6).

Reversives

This could be considered under the category of equivalents, but I have listed it separately because it is a special type. The one expression is the opposite of the other. For example, if we are talking about our dying and rising with Christ we can express the truth in terms of reversives as follows: "We *died* with Christ"/"We *live* with Christ."

A very clear example occurs in Galatians 6:7–8. After the introductory words, "A man reaps what he sows," Paul writes:

The one who sows   to please his sinful nature,
                    from that nature   will reap   destruction.
The one who sows   to please the Spirit,
                    from that Spirit   will reap   eternal life.

When the members of the sentence are set out in this way, the pattern becomes obvious. The words, "The one who sows" and "will reap," are repeated in identical form. The reversives are "sinful nature" versus "Spirit," and "destruction" versus "eternal life." There is also an inner structure here, employing the device of equivalents. This involves the repetition of "sinful nature" in the first member, introduced first by "please his" and then by "from that." In the second member the repeated word is "Spirit." Thus two literary patterns are found, one within the other. However, it is the larger pattern, utilizing the reversives, which will be of most use for the preacher. It provides a very simple, but powerful outline.

Reciprocals

In this case, it is not the substitution of an element in a phrase that is the reverse of another, as in the previous example, but rather two phrases that are reciprocal in nature. We might say, for example, that Christ died for all (first member) and that as a result we live for him (second member). There is a good biblical example in 1 Corinthians 3:6. Here the first member is double. It can be written out as follows:

	I	planted	the seed	
	Apollos	watered	it	
but	God	made	it	grow.

We can see another example in James 4:7 and 8. "Resist the devil/ and he will flee from you." Also: "Come near to God/and he will come near to you." Actually there is also a larger pattern here, a compositional one of contrast. The first member deals with our relationship (or nonrelationship) to the devil and the second deals with our relationship to God. Here also we have fine structural material for a sermon.

Alliterations and Other Patterns of Sound

Alliteration is too well known to need any explanation or example. The problem is that what we see in the Greek will probably have no corresponding feature in the English text. If we do happen upon an alliteration, even though we may not be able to use it as such in a sermon, it can alert us to a special emphasis by the author. We should also be alert, though, to other patterns of sound. We noticed above the two words at the beginning of the Book of Hebrews that have similar sound: πολυμερῶς, πολυτρόπως. Originally the Epistles were heard rather than read, so this would have been very striking. In the same book there is a superb example that also functions to set the Old Testament and New Testament revelations in contrast. The author describes coming to Mount Sinai as to a mountain "that is burning with fire; to darkness, gloom and storm" (12:18). The Christian believer, in contrast, comes to "Mount Zion," where there are "thousands upon thousands of angels in joyful assembly." But it is not only the vocabulary that illustrates the contrast, it is the sound of the words that describe the experience at Mount Sinai (v. 18) that produce part of the effect. This is partly achieved by stringing along a number of words connected by the repeating καὶ ("and"), and by including two words of ominous and similar sound, as follows: ψηλαφωμένῳ [ὄρει] καὶ κεκαυμένῳ πυρὶ καὶ γνόφῳ καὶ ζόφῳ καὶ θυέλλῃ καὶ σάλπιγγος ἤχῳ καὶ φωνῇ ῥημάτων. If I were preaching from this passage, I might even say aloud the words, καὶ γνόφῳ καὶ ζόφῳ (kai gnophō kai zophō) to give the congregation something of a feel for the pattern of sound. Certainly we can also take note of the overall contrast that the author has made between verses 18–21 and verses 22–24.

Word Frequency

This is not a "pattern" as such, except where words may be repeated in close proximity to each other. It is good to be alert to frequent uses of words, although this also presents some hazards. One danger is to assume that because a word is repeated it indicates the "theme" of a book or section. Many commentators and preachers have assumed that the theme of Philippians is "joy" because of the frequency of that noun and of the verb "rejoice." This is certainly a characteristic of Philippians, but, as we noted above, a consideration of other terminology shows that "mental attitude" is an even more prominent theme. The question is not only what words appear frequently but how they are used, whether related terms also appear, and whether or not they occur in contexts that clearly express the major thrust of the book.

An instance of word patterns occurs in 1 Timothy 1:5 and 19. In verse 5 Paul speaks of "a good conscience and a sincere faith." In verse 19 the order is reversed and he speaks of "faith and a good conscience." This phenomenon in itself would not prove anything, but when we recognize that the epistle is concerned with maintaining the faith at a time when it is being threatened, and also about the importance of morality when that is being undermined, we see that the repetition of these words in fairly close proximity has significance.

Study of word frequency in the Gospels is especially productive, in that it helps us to perceive the particular theological emphasis of each Gospel. In addition to the statistical compilations of Hawkins[21] and of Morgenthaler,[22] one recent computer-assisted work has been especially useful to me. That is *Horae Synopticae*

Electronicae by L. Gaston.[23] This work not only lists the number of times a word is used in the Gospels, but it breaks it down according to the types of materials and alleged editorial units in the Gospels. Some of this is more useful to those who engage in literary criticism of the Gospels. However it has great usefulness also for those whose main interest is expository preaching. One unique characteristic of this work is that the word usage is statistically analyzed in such a way as to indicate when frequent occurrences are really significant.

Chapter Six

The Facts:
The Final Touches

Emotional Color Patterns

In our electronic age we have become used to hearing electronic games and other gadgets that simulate the human voice. We also hear parodies of this on radio and television. The electronic voice is typically flat, impersonal, and without expression. Unfortunately we sometimes read and interpret Scripture to others in a similar lifeless way. We have been so programmed to do "grammatico-historical" exegesis, that we miss the "forest" of literary characteristics and emotional color while analyzing the syntactical "trees." But Scripture came through men, not angels, as they were moved by the Holy Spirit. They wrote with all of the passion that they were feeling at the moment. In fact, in some instances, their emotional feelings became part of their work, not accidentally, but deliberately.

Look, for example, at Paul's Letter to the Galatians. We are familiar with the fact that Paul used strong language at the opening of this epistle. We usually note the words at the end of verse 8, "let him be eternally condemned!" "Condemned" (ἀνάθεμα) is indeed a strong word in itself, but its force is further strengthened by the context. Note also the word that begins this paragraph, θαυμάζω, "I am astonished." Paul airs his emotions for all to see. He then continues in the next paragraph by using such words as καθ' ὑπερβολὴν, "intensely" (v. 13), and περισσοτέρως ζηλωτὴς, "extremely zealous" (v. 14). Chapter 2 describes Paul's opposition of Peter, surely an emotional confrontation. Chapter 3 opens with the words, "You foolish Galatians! Who has bewitched you?" Paul repeats the word "foolish" in verse 3. Also in this paragraph (3:1–5) Paul uses a series of rhetorical questions. This device carries an emotional communication as well as a logical one. In verse 15 he uses the term "Brothers." This in itself constitutes an appeal to emotion. In chapter 4 Paul appeals to their earlier feelings for him. Just prior to this section (vv. 12–16), he says with great feeling, "I fear for you, that somehow I have wasted my efforts on you" (v. 11). The "efforts" of which he speaks began on his prior visit with them, which he will now proceed to describe.

He begins the section with an attempt to persuade the Galatians to identify with him as he does with them. He strengthens this appeal with the words, "Brothers, I appeal to you" (ἀδελφοί, δέομαι ὑμῶν, 4:12). Then he says, "You have done me no wrong." He goes on to refer to his earlier illness (vv. 13–14). He says that even though his illness was a "trial" to them, they did not treat him "with contempt or scorn" (οὐκ ἐξουθενήσατε οὐδὲ ἐξεπτύσατε). These are also strong words, and there may also be a play on the sound of the prefix, ἐξ. In contrast he reminds them that they welcomed him, "as if I were an angel of God, as if I were Christ Jesus himself." The expositor should not stumble over whether this is an overdrawn exaggeration or not. He should recognize in it a tremendously emotional appeal in which the apostle is trying to stir the memories of the Galatians as to how they felt about him when he first preached the gospel there. If Paul can only rekindle that original feeling, he will have gone a long way towards winning them back from the heretics who are presently troubling them. He spells this out in verse 15, "What has happened to all your joy?" Note the "color" word, "joy." Now he reaches the peak of his emotional argument, that, if they could have done it, "you would have torn out your eyes and given them to me." Paul is not only arousing pity here, but he is trying to get them to identify with him so closely that their present attitude would not only be unthinkable logically, but impossible emotionally. He therefore concludes in verse 16, "Have I now become your enemy by telling you the truth?"

The following paragraph (vv. 17–20) continues this contrast of identification versus alienation. He uses the word for being zealous three times (ζηλόω). He says that the heretics want to "alienate" (ἐκκλεῖσαι) the Galatians from Paul. Paul follows with that beautiful appeal, "My dear children, for whom I am again in the pains of childbirth until Christ is formed in you, how I wish I could be with you now and change my tone, because I am perplexed about you!" (vv. 19–20). The rest of the epistle continues to argue strongly and emotionally, frequently using the word "Brother" as an element of the appeal.

I have gone into considerable detail to show how important emotional "color" is in this epistle. The expositor of Galatians who only gives a cool, logical explanation of justification by faith has evacuated the epistle of its impact.

I suggested above that we may need to question the theme of "joy" as the subject of Philippians. Nevertheless, even if joy is not the key theme as such, it is certainly a vibrant emotional color, which ought to be faithfully conveyed in a sermon on the book. (There are other emotional "colors" in Philippians also, which are there for the alert reader.) Paul's frequent use of the word "boast" (καυχάομαι), which includes positive (Romans 5:2, 3, 11), negative (Romans 2:17, 23; 3:27), and sarcastic (2 Corinthians 11:16–33; cf. 10:12–18) feelings, exemplifies both literary and emotional "color."

Other illustrations of emotional "color" patterns will easily come to mind. They include such feelings as hope, anticipation, fear, confidence, loneliness, and love, to name only a few. James reminds us that Elijah was a man "just like us" (ὁμοιοπαθής), having the same feelings as we do. Likewise, when we preach we should, in effect, be assuring our congregation that the authors of Scripture and the people who appear on the sacred pages are just like us. We tend to think that recourse to emotion is a human device for homiletical manipulation. I would like to suggest that more properly this emotional dimension can and should be drawn from Scripture itself as part of the exposition. This will both keep us from missing what Scripture contains and caution us against introducing emotional aspects to our sermon that are not appropriate to the passage being expounded.

A great deal could be said about the emotional life of our Lord Jesus Christ. It is difficult for translations to bring out the intensity of his emotions. One example of this is in John 11:33, where the English text will say something like, "He was deeply moved in spirit and troubled." That is a good translation, but hardly as strong as the Greek, ἐνεβριμήσατο τῷ πνεύματι καὶ ἐτάραξεν ἑαυτόν. This conveys far more than the much quoted "Jesus wept" two verses later. One gets the impression that Jesus was deeply disturbed, not only because his friend had died, but because of the evil that brought death into the world, because of the unbelief all around him, and because of the effect of this death on others whom he loved. If the Lord Jesus had emotions that ran this deep we should not fear to convey something of the emotional "color" of his life as well as of the other personages of Scripture.

Underlying Assumptions

In recent years grammarians have given attention to what is called "transformational grammar" and to "deep structure." Stated briefly, deep structure is the basic affirmation that underlies the complex structures that lie on the surface of a text. Skipping the technicalities, I should like to show how some of these insights can be useful to the preacher. If we say, "The sermon that the pastor preached was sent out on cassette tapes," two "kernel" affirmations lie below the surface. One is that the pastor preached the sermon; the second is that the sermon was distributed in tape form. The words, "The wrecked car was sold," indicate two passives, which are transformations of two active affirmations. Someone wrecked the car and then someone sold the car. In the sentence, "His uncle's death affected the boy deeply," there is embedded in the first part the affirmation that his uncle died.

We see from such illustrations that language has a way of accommodating various affirmations in modified structures. This is often done for variety and sometimes for brevity. The point to keep in mind is that information that *we assume* may be *new* to the *hearer.* If I say, "His uncle's death . . . ," I am speaking as though the death of the uncle is assumed. But (speaking theoretically) someone may be listening to me who knew the boy's uncle and is shocked to learn that he has died. To take a more complex example, an entire relative clause can express an assumption that the speaker or writer makes, and which is known by perhaps most of his audience, but which may be unknown to some. Imagine a person who has been stranded on a desert island for a number of years, who, on his return to civilization, sees a headline, "Astronauts Who Landed on Mars Return Safely." If this former castaway had not known that astronauts were planning to go to Mars, the "news" for him would not be that the astronauts *returned* safely but that astronauts had *gone to Mars*! The relative clause, "who landed on Mars," thus is an assumption in form, but may be new information to the reader.

Now let us apply this to an important biblical phrase, "through the death of his Son" (Romans 5:10). The death of God's Son is basic to Christian theology. Christian readers of Romans 5 are already aware of this. However a missionary seeking to take the gospel to another culture may need to explain such a phrase very carefully. The deep structure would be something like this: "God had a Son"; "The Son died"; "This act was instrumental in nature" (implied in the word "through"). My suggestion is that, as we prepare a text for preaching, we ask ourselves what affirmations lie below the surface structure that may be "news" to someone in the congregation. We do not need to go through the grammatical exercise of dissecting the sentence into small kernels. We do need to be sure, however, that we probe the depth of each sentence and each clause, keeping in mind the probable knowledge level of our congregation.

Even apart from grammatical structure there are evidences of underlying assumptions. Sometimes we need to ask ourselves what doctrines or other facts are understood by speakers and hearers in a narrative or author and reader in an epistle. The most obvious example of this is found in 2 Corinthians and 2 Thessalonians, where the previous visits and correspondence were occasions of sharing certain truths that are then assumed in the subsequent correspondence. But even where we have just one conversation or letter, we must be alert for common assumptions. Are there some assumptions that I should explain to my congregation to help them understand the passage at hand? This is especially important in evangelistic messages.

Our task in exposition goes much further than just finding points for a sermon outline. It is, as we saw at the very beginning, to *explain* a passage and to apply it appropriately. This explanation and application may require extra time and work on a phrase or even a word that holds the key to the understanding of the major clauses.

This section has been a relatively brief one, but it could have benefits far beyond its size if it makes our exposition richer and more faithful to the text.

Thrust of the Passage

It may seem to counter all that has been said thus far about probing the depths of a passage in detail, but I am now suggesting that our next step be to determine the basic thrust and teaching of this passage and to express it in a *single sentence*. However, the need for a summary statement is certainly apparent at this point. The very fact that exegesis involves us in a search for meaning in even the smallest elements of a sentence means that our sermon preparation up to this point may tend to be atomistic. What we need now is cohesion and direction. It may take a considerable amount of time to reduce everything that I have learned from the passage to one sentence, but it will be worth it. People usually do not leave a church service meditating on a number of different facts that they have learned from the sermon. It is far more likely that if the sermon has had focus they will carry away *one basic impression* and will know what it is that God expects them to do in response to the message. If the sermon has not had focus, they may have some general feelings and impressions, but these will not be sharply defined or motivational in their lives. The people who tell a pastor after his message that they "enjoyed" it because they learned so much, just possibly might be the very ones who need not more information but a heavy dose of application. Great as the famine of the Word of God is in our land, the solution is not to provide a smorgasbord of biblical information, but a balanced diet that corresponds to nutritional needs.

It is certainly true that the Holy Spirit can take an assortment of truths garnered from a passage and apply them as needed in individual hearts. We need to be humble before God in the realization that only the Spirit knows what these needs are. I shall never forget the time an alcoholic found just the biblical message he needed from a verse I mentioned, almost in passing, in the Book of Habakkuk. Nevertheless, if a passage has a main thrust in its teaching and in its application, I am responsible to God to present that in balance and in clarity. If I do this, surely the component parts of that passage will be seen in their proper place and with the proper perspective. Therefore, I strongly urge the discipline of making such a statement in a single sentence that summarizes the teaching of the passage. If the passage contains a narrative, I will summarize the event and its significance. For example, my summary of Acts 11:1–18 might be, "Peter related the conversion of Cornelius to the Jewish believers in Jerusalem, explaining how God prepared him through a vision to accept a Gentile, how God brought him and Cornelius together, and how the Holy Spirit came upon Cornelius, in order that the Jewish Christians might realize that God was bringing Gentiles to himself." Admittedly this is a long sentence! I would certainly not use it in a message. However, by expressing it all in one sentence, I have forced myself to relate the various parts together syntactically. That means that I cannot simply set several statements in individual sentences alongside of each other without showing their inner connection. One sentence means one continuous line of thought. This disciplines me to see the passage as a whole.

PART III | APPLYING THE TEXT

Chapter Seven # Determining the Application: The "Function"

There are two ways of determining the function of a sermon. We might call these ways (1) from "Above" and (2) from "Below," that is (1) from the divinely given text and (2) from the needs of the congregation. I am obviously exaggerating a bit and making these seem to be exclusive of each other. But the fact is that some expository messages seem, at least, to show little awareness of the real needs of the congregation. At the other extreme are those sermons that develop their application from the needs of the congregation with little regard to the original function of the passage. The former method leads to irrelevance; the latter, to distortion.

It can certainly be argued that if I am preaching with passion to the real needs of a congregation, God will use his Word in my sermon, even if it is poorly expounded. It could also be argued that if I teach the Word of God clearly and prayerfully, God will speak through his Word and meet needs, even though I fumble in making the application. But why can I not determine the application of the passage *both* from the life setting of the text *and* from the present needs of the congregation? It is this dual approach to application that I want to pursue further in this chapter.

Review the Life Setting of the Passage

Just as this is one of the first steps in the exegesis of a passage, so it should be one of the first steps in the application of that passage. When we are seeking a principle, or, as it is sometimes called, a timeless truth,[24] we must remember that the full meaning and significance of this truth must be derived from and clearly seen in the context of the biblical passage. That truth may be a statement of theology (an eternal truth about God, his ways, and his work), or it may express a truth about the ideals God seeks in our lives and the response God seeks from us. I should be able to express this truth in a statement that, because it is not limited in its application, does not contain any proper name except that of God himself. It is important to realize that for such a principle or statement to bridge the gap between the biblical passage and present circumstances, it must be solidly rooted in the actual circumstances of the context of the passage.

An example of the above that we will all recognize would be the truth: "God will provide for all our needs abundantly." This truth finds expression in two passages, 2 Corinthians 9:8 and Philippians 4:19. When we study the life setting of each passage, however, we see that the recipients of the letter had given generously to the needs of others. The "timeless truth" therefore has to be rooted in "time," that is, in the situation in which it was expressed. Our application must then be rigorously made to a similar life situation, in which God's people are giving sacrificially to help others in need. The following questions are helpful:

What Circumstances or Needs Were Addressed?

As I am writing these lines I cannot help but think of a missionary letter I read earlier today. The letter rehearsed the missionary's search for guidance from the Lord regarding a contemplated move. She quoted a number of verses from various parts of the Scripture, and expressed her perplexity as to how these verses were to be fulfilled in her life. Several of the verses related specifically to historical circumstances in the Old Testament and had absolutely no bearing on her situation. In no case did she refer to the context, either biblically or historically, and it is no wonder that she had trouble in making the proper application. Unfortunately this use of the Bible is all too typical. We can be thankful that God sometimes speaks to us in spite of our poor hermeneutics! That, however, is no excuse for the preacher mishandling the Word of God and setting a bad example.

What we should be doing is to enter the life of the people involved in a biblical narrative, or of those to whom a biblical epistle is addressed, and acquaint ourselves thoroughly with the circumstances. When I begin to ask how people felt, what their needs were, why they needed a word from God or the particular ministry that was given them, and whether there is anything here that corresponds to our contemporary situation, I am beginning to bridge the chasm of the centuries.

What Purpose Did the Passage Serve?

Here I am asking not only what happened and why God acted in the way he did (assuming for the moment that we are dealing with a narrative), but also why the event is recorded in Scripture. In the case of an epistle, we may simply ask why this paragraph was included in the letter. To put it another way, we reverently ask God, "Why did you put this here?" I am not only asking what the teaching *is* but *why* it is given here. At times the answer will be very clear from the context preceding and following. Sometimes the passage itself speaks so loudly that there is no ambiguity. There are other times, however, when I must exercise careful judgment based on what I know of the general direction of a book and of the purposes for which God inspired Scripture as a whole. Here I find 2 Timothy 3:16–17 very helpful: "All scripture is God-breathed and is useful for teaching, rebuking, correcting and training in righteousness, so that the man of God may be thoroughly equipped for every good work." Paul probably did not intend to exhaust all of the functions of Scripture in this one verse, but it certainly outlines the varied purposes for which God inspired his Word. Personally I like to bring this passage to whatever biblical text I am studying and allow it to guide me in understanding the purpose and function of that text. I know that the passage in 2 Timothy provides help for understanding the *present* application of Scripture, but it can hardly be any less relevant for the understanding of the purpose for which a biblical text was *originally* written. Why did Mark include this particular incident? Why did Luke record that phase of Paul's missionary journey? Why does the Book of Revelation narrate these fearsome events? For what purpose did James include those difficult verses? These are the kinds of questions I should be asking at this point.

What Immediate Results Did the Author Seek?

This question may sound very much like the preceding one, but it carries the matter a step further. Now we are thinking about the intended outcome. We may use the parable of the Sower (Matthew 13; Mark 4; Luke 8) as an illustration. The *circumstances* are to be found in the ministry of Jesus and the varied responses he was receiving. These included the hostility described in Matthew 12 and Mark 3 that resulted in Jesus' saying about the unpardonable sin. As to the *purpose*, Jesus apparently told the parable, including the interpretation, in order to explain why the responses to his ministry varied so, and also to encourage the disciples. The *result* he sought would seem to have been self-examination and faith on the part of the crowds who heard him, and a realistic optimism and perseverance on the part of the disciples. For an illustration from the Epistles, we may look at 1 Timothy 3:16, that magnificent passage on the "mystery of godliness." The circumstances were that Timothy needed not only instruction but encouragement from Paul. As we observed earlier, Paul is emphasizing "a good conscience and a good faith" (1:5, 19). Timothy is to teach the truth and to be a good example (4:12, 15–16). Inclusion of the great creedal statement of 3:16, with its emphasis on the vindication of the risen Christ in heaven and on earth, is apparently for the purpose of encouraging Timothy to be faithful to the truth of the Lord Jesus. The result that Paul sought was apparently a freedom from fear coupled with great liberty and power in Timothy's ministry. First Timothy 3:16, therefore, should not be taught simply as an isolated creedal statement. Paul expected it to have an *effect* in Timothy's ministry.

Sometimes the circumstances, purpose, and desired effect of a passage of Scripture are so clear as to be unmistakable. Second Peter 3 comes to mind: Scoffers will say, "Where is this 'coming' he promised?" The circumstances are clear from this. So are the purpose and desired effect: "Since everything will be destroyed in this way, what kind of people ought you to be? You ought to live holy and godly lives as you look forward to the day of God and speed its coming." Other passages, not so clear, will require more study, but is that not the pastor's great delight?

Describe the Function of the Original Text With a Word or Phrase

Having determined the circumstances, purpose, and desired effect of a passage, it is time for us to move away from the original circumstance and determine how it can match our contemporary circumstance, which rarely have many particulars in common with biblical history. It is at this point that we run into the danger of abstraction. I believe that the more vivid and concrete we can make the function of a passage in its original life setting appear to the congregation, the more effective the application of that text will be. When Jesus wanted to cause people to "always pray and not give up," he did not merely state an abstract principle. He told a parable.

Nevertheless, there are certain categories of function, ways in which Scripture serves its purpose, that fit both a number of biblical passages and also typical circumstances in life today. Suppose we take a passage mentioned above, 2 Peter 3. Peter's teaching about the destruction of the elements and the certainty of judgment, along with his words about holy living could be described as "motivational," "exhorting," or "warning." Likewise Jesus' words about people praying and not giving up can be described as "motivational," "exhorting," or "encouraging." These categories are often overlapping.

I am going to give a list of these possible categories. I shall not provide examples in each case, since they are self-explanatory and undoubtedly various passages will come to mind. One of them, however, may not be clear: "Showing cause-effect relationships." I have in mind here the sort of series in Romans 1 where Paul says that he is eager to preach the gospel *because* of his sense of obligation (vv. 14–15), he is not ashamed of the gospel *because* it is God's power for salvation (v. 16), the gospel does issue in salvation *because* God's righteousness is revealed in it (v. 17), the wrath of God is revealed against godlessness *since* people had evidence of God and are without excuse for rejecting it (vv. 18–20), God gave people over to lusts and impurity *because* of their attitudes and actions (vv. 31–32), and so on.

Here then is a list of functions, occasionally overlapping, and certainly not exhaustive:

Motivational

Perhaps the best example of this is 2 Corinthians 5:9–11 and 14–15, where Paul says that he himself was motivated by fear (relating to the judgment seat of Christ) and by love (the love of Christ in dying for him). Another example would be the rewards and deprivations mentioned in the Beatitudes and Woes of Matthew 5 and Luke 6. In Ephesians 5:5 Paul warns that immoral people will be excluded from the kingdom, and in verse 6 he further warns that such will incur the wrath of God. Again 2 Peter 3:11 says that we should be motivated to live holy lives by the anticipation of the destruction that will come upon the heavens and the elements.

Convicting

One naturally thinks of the early chapters of Romans for passages that bring conviction. We should also turn to the Gospels, where we find strong words of the Lord Jesus in such passages as Matthew 5:13, 19, 22, and 32, to name just a few. There are also sayings imbedded in narratives that bring conviction, such as Luke 10:41–42 and also sayings given in the context of parables, such as Luke 16:13.

Comforting, Encouraging

Once again we think of the Beatitudes. Also 2 Corinthians 1:3–7 belongs in this category. It is not only an expression of Paul's own feelings, but a statement intended to encourage his readers. Hebrews 10:19–25 uses the truth of the high priesthood of the Lord Jesus Christ as a means of encouragement and also of exhortation to his readers to encourage one another. We may also think of entire books, such as 1 Peter and Revelation, which were written in part at least, to encourage people undergoing persecution.

Proclaiming the Gospel

Here I am thinking of passages whose *function* in context is to proclaim the gospel, not just passages that can be retooled and *made into* gospel illustrations. Unfortunately many Christians tend to memorize and quote Romans 3:23, "for all have sinned . . . ," in isolation from the rest of the passage, going to other passages for further aspects of the gospel message. But the gospel is fully expressed in this very paragraph!

In the Book of Acts there are several speeches that present the gospel clearly and directly. This was their *function* when originally preached. They perform that function in Acts also, for Luke probably wrote Acts (and the Gospel) for a combination of purposes, one of which is to present and defend the gospel message. A Hellenistic non-Christian reading Acts would have been enthralled by the stories in it which, in their literary form, would have reminded him of some of the novels he was used to reading. But here was a book that conveyed true history. In progressing through it, with all its exciting stories of travel and even shipwreck, the reader would come across speeches that brought the gospel to his heart. One such speech is in Acts 13, with its statements, "We tell you the good news" (v. 32) and "I want you to know that through Jesus the forgiveness of sins is proclaimed to you" (v. 38). Another example is the well known Areopagus address of chapter 17, in which Paul marvelously (in a speech not even part of a planned evangelistic mission) presents the truth of God as Creator, as Lord of history, and as Judge. He speaks of Jesus' resurrection (which surely implies that he spoke of his atoning death), and of the coming day of reckoning. How many evangelistic messages today contain so much solid doctrinal foundation for the gospel?

Leading to Worship

The first passage that probably comes to mind is Revelation 4:1–5:14. Here is a sequence of ascriptions of praise to God for his nature and attributes (4:8), and for his creative works (4:11) and then of adoration of the Lord Jesus Christ, the slain Lamb (5:9–14). Surely John intended his readers to join in that chorus of praise. The same can be said for other doxologies in Revelation, such as 7:12 and 11:17–18. There are passages in the Epistles that also lead to worship, perhaps the best known being Romans 11:33–36. In the Gospels and Acts, there are statements about the work of Christ and of the Holy Spirit that issue in doxology. The healing of the paralytic in Luke 5:17–26 has its climax in praise. See also the healing in Acts 3:1–10. Luke seems deeply concerned to lead his readers to worship; his narratives have this element more prominently than those in Matthew and Mark.

Setting Standards

The concerned pastor desires to set forth clear standards of holy living, yet often hesitates to preach lists of dos and don'ts. It is good here to let Scripture do the work. The Sermon on the Mount is an obvious source of moral standards, for this is a primary function of the Sermon. Ephesians 4–5 provide standards also, and do so by way of contrast with the old ways of life characterized by pagan debauchery. Other passages from the epistle will easily come to mind.

Setting Goals

An outstanding example of this is Ephesians 1. I referred earlier to the list of expressions of purpose that characterize the opening paragraphs of Ephesians. Other passages would certainly include Matthew 6:24 (about choosing between God and money), and 6:33 (about seeking first God and his righteousness). Also Jesus' summary of the Law in Mark 12:31–34 and parallels appropriately serves as a guide to proper goals that will please God (cf. Romans 13:6–10). Passages like 1 Corinthians 10:31 (". . . whether you eat or drink . . . do it all to the glory of God"), Romans 14:19 (". . . do what leads to peace and to mutual edification") are intended to establish goals for Christian behavior.

Dealing With Doctrinal Issues

It need only be said that if we preach on a specific doctrine, we will do best by selecting a passage in which that doctrine is a primary subject. It is not always necessary to go to the main passage on a doctrine (it well may have been covered in a recent sermon), but I should at least look for a passage that clearly teaches that doctrine rather than alluding to it obliquely.

Dealing With Problems

This is a touchy area, and it is obvious that our word from the pulpit will generally be more acceptable if the Scripture is appropriate and speaks for itself. It will probably be good to take a passage that not only speaks to the problem, but that also shows how the problem has been, or can be worked out. A typical passage in this respect would be Acts 6:1–7, which shows how the early church dealt with a problem of division and suspicion.

Showing Cause-effect Relationship

These are passages that provide an explanation for a state of being. They help us to understand why things are as they are. Romans 1 is a prime example. The degenerate state of humankind exists because the rejection of God and his truth resulted in God giving people up to various expressions of immorality. The whole first chapter of Romans is a study in cause-effect relationships.

Laying a Foundation for Faith or Action

We often urge people to take certain steps, but if we fail to provide solid reasons and assurances, we may leave them paralyzed and feeling guilty over their inactivity. A well-known example is Romans 1:16, "I am not ashamed of the gospel, because it is the power of God . . . ." The "because" not only expresses causality, but also is an undergirding support for Paul's confidence. So also in Colossians 2:9, Paul tells the Colossians not to look elsewhere for spiritual truth: "*For* in Christ all the fullness of the Deity lives in bodily form." Once again, the emphasis is not on causality, but on the *reason* for action, a basic foundational fact on which one can base decision and action.

Giving Perspective on Life

A good deal of Scripture provides new insights not only about God himself, but about ourselves and our world. These give us a perspective on our lives as they are lived in the course of history. Ephesians, for example, displays God's purposes in the church and opens our minds to the realization that God's intent is that "now, through the church, the manifold wisdom of God should be made known to the rulers and authorities in the heavenly realms" (Ephesians 3:10). This not only expresses divine purpose (see above on "goals"), but also opens new vistas to us of the role of the church in the present age. The stage-by-stage unfolding of God's "mystery," his designs in history, also provides insight and an awareness that there is a front side to the tapestry of life that, as we view it, so to speak, from the back, appears so tangled. Prophecy has this as one of its functions throughout Scripture.

Teaching Ethics

For a long time evangelicals taught Scripture but neglected ethics, while many others taught ethics but lacked a biblical basis. The ideal, of course, is to teach ethics from Scripture. Some passages do this by precept, some by personal example, some through parable. The parable of the dishonest steward, for example, takes an "earthy" situation and through it shows how the Christian can be faithful in stewardship without being trapped by greed (Luke 16:1–13). The Sermon on the Mount is full of ethical injunctions. Also Jesus' placing of human need above ceremonial obligations provides a model for us. But once again, it is important to pay attention to the *function* of the passage in its context, lest we wrest out of context and misapply verses that we think teach ethical opinions we have actually developed on our own. The story in Luke 5:27–32 about Jesus at Levi's banquet, for example, with the complaint that Jesus ate and drank with sinners, does not have as its function to teach that Christians today either should or should not partake of alcoholic beverages with non-Christians, but to show Jesus' gracious association with sinners for their salvation.

Other categories could be suggested that are common and self-evident. There are Scriptures that have as their function to correct, to engender concern (social or missionary) for others, to provide guidance, and to give warnings. Examples will quickly suggest themselves. The important point to realize is that this is not just a list of *topics*, but a list of *functions*. That is, we are not merely looking for verses that touch on this or that topic, but for passages that have a certain purpose or function as their very reason for inclusion in the canon. The discipline of determining the contextual function of a passage cannot be neglected, for it is a *primary link between exposition and application*.

This list can now become not only a means of bridging the chasm between the biblical life situation and our own, but also a means of helping the preacher achieve variety in his sermons. I suspect that if some of us were asked to categorize our sermons over the past several years according to this list, we would find that our sermons would tend to fall into just a few of the categories, and that few or none of them fall into some of the others. Contemplation of this list can also help a pastor evaluate his ministry as a whole. Undoubtedly there will be a strong correlation between style of pastoral ministry and type of sermon. Whether in the pulpit, in committee meeting, or in private conversation, some will tend to encourage and others to exhort. The ministry of some pastors is very problem centered, others consciously endeavor to help Christians mature. Some have rarely thought of helping congregations, committees, or individuals to set goals, but talk a great deal about standards and doctrines. If a pastor is "giving perspective on life" he will find that his exhortations are more readily understood and therefore accepted.

Of course we cannot fit every biblical passage into one of these categories. Some passages will have more than one function. Some will not have any single obvious function in themselves, but will contribute to the purpose of the book as a whole. Others will provide supporting or ancillary material for topics that are treated more centrally elsewhere. The point of this list is to help us to become more conscious of *what is appropriate and what is not* in our attempt to apply Scripture to current needs.

Consider the Needs of the Congregation

The following are just some of the situations and needs that exist in any congregation:

> Personal needs (anxiety, loneliness, grief, depression, spiritual dryness, need for guidance, etc.).
>
> Corporate moods (economic concerns, discouragement, conflict, lack of enthusiasm in the church, shock over a recent death in the congregation, apprehension over a planned building program, etc.).
>
> Current social or ethical situations (among Christians or in the community).
>
> Public crises (elections, assassination attempts, international problems, accident in community, etc.).
>
> Spiritual milestones in the life of the church.
>
> Spiritual state of special groups (new believers, elderly, youth, those in mid-life crisis, singles, married, divorced, etc.).
>
> Ongoing needs for edification and instruction.

The reader who is a pastor will readily identify with the concerns listed above. The seminary student, on the other hand, will need to grow in his sensitivity to such needs. It is in this sense that a sermon comes from "below," as mentioned earlier. Some will select the Scripture text for a sermon according to the need of the hour. The expositor who is already preaching through a book or series of books should keep in mind the previous list of functions, and to be sure that he is alert to the potential of each passage to meet the needs of the congregation. The seminary student who comes to the pulpit fresh from exciting classes in church history, biblical studies, theology, and so on, has to get used to the fact (even though he may already be well informed of it) that not all worshipers come to the service with their minds in the heavenlies. The more keenly he is aware of congregational needs the more readily his congregation will respond to the teaching of the Scriptures.

This raises a question that cannot be answered at length but that calls for some comment. How can the preacher be aware of his people's needs? The conscientious preacher feels the need to spend many hours in preparation. Paper work, committees, community tasks, and many other needs consume his time. The visitation of church families as a matter of course has been abandoned by many busy pastors. How then is he to know their needs? In my opinion the call to expository preaching is also a call to pastoral ministry. Therefore the preacher *must* find ways to be close to the people. Even if others on the church staff and in the congregation carry on most of the visitation, the preacher needs to seek as much contact with the people as possible. He can also learn from his associates (for example in weekly staff meetings) what the feelings, needs, and problems are among the flock. Asking the right questions and *listening* are imperative. If the preacher is not personally aware of the needs of his own congregation, his sermons may have little personal relevance to them.

Apply the Passage to the Needs

The procedure is now obvious: (1) Consider which of the *needs* we are aware of truly correspond to the *original purpose* and *function* of the passage chosen. If a passage is not already selected, we can move from the need to an appropriate passage. (2) Prayerfully determine what *message* God desires to convey through your ministry at this time. (3) In faith decide what *objectives* you can trust God to fulfill through this passage. (4) Construct the message from the passage, making sure that the original *intention* and *balance* of the passage is in no way distorted by your application.

This procedure should help the pastor in what may seem the most difficult part of his sermon preparation: choosing the topic. When we are overwhelmed by a great number of needs to which we feel burdened to speak, it is hard to know which to select for emphasis. And even when we have determined some order of priority according to which these needs might be addressed, we still have to select topics and texts that will enable us to deal with them. But when we are preaching expositionally, we have some assistance in this difficult decision. If we are preaching through a book, we can bring each chapter or section to bear on whatever needs we sense to be pressing that are dealt with in the passage. Over the course of a number of weeks, a variety of topics will yield themselves from the successive passages.

Let us review those four steps just mentioned. The first was to match the *function* of a passage to the *needs* of a congregation. Whether the passage is determined in advance as part of a series, or whether it is selected to meet a need, I must be sure that I am not forcing the passage to fulfill a purpose or perform a function for which it is not suited. Once again, at the risk of repetition, the context is as important in determining the purpose and function of a passage as it is in determining its interpretation.

The second step was to determine prayerfully what *message* God desires to convey through the preaching of this passage. The message is God's living Word today. It requires a holy, sensitive, and obedient preacher, who will let the text both inform and master him, and who will be an instrument through whom the text will speak to others. The message is more than a text and more than a topic. It is God's voice to us.

Third, we noted that we should exercise faith in deciding what *objectives* God wants to accomplish through his Word. That is, we should have a clear picture of what response the congregation should make to the message. This requires faith that God's Word will indeed accomplish the purpose for which he gave it. It also requires that we pray earnestly not only for our delivery of the message but for the people and their response to it. I am convinced that we would see God work in even greater power than we do, if we would identify more clearly the objectives we expect God's Word to fulfill and pray in faith for that fulfillment.

Fourth, when we proceed to the actual structuring of the message, we must be sure to preserve the original *intention* and *balance* of the passage. It is not by whim that the discussion of the form of the message comes in this book *after* discussion on its function. In most instances, form should follow the flow of the biblical narrative or argument.

Although this has been only a brief discussion of the function and application of Scripture to the needs of the congregation, nevertheless, it is just here that we must be strongly emphatic, because it is so easy for Bible expositors to fail at this point. At the risk of overemphasis, we must remind ourselves that unless we have made a sensitive, compassionate, forceful, and unmistakable application, we have merely done exposition, not expository *preaching.* We must constantly be asking ourselves not only *what* we are preaching, but *why.* In 1 Timothy 1:5 Paul says, "The goal of this command is love . . . ." We need to ask ourselves repeatedly what the *goal* of our exposition is.

I like to picture myself taking the members of my congregation with me back into biblical times. We stand as invisible observers of the life situation of the text. We identify with the needs and concerns of those who listened to the Lord Jesus, of those who heard the first reading of one of Paul's letters, of those beleaguered Christians who read the Book of Revelation. We think together not only of what they felt, but of why they felt that way. We learn how the ministry of the Lord Jesus and of the apostles or of other writers of the New Testament helped them. We talk together about our world, and about how we feel. We may think of Illinois instead of Palestine; of an energy management company instead of a carpenter's shop; of a modern hospital instead of a seashore; of dollars instead of drachmas. We do not rush to platitudes and principles. When we talk about "timeless truths," we must recognize that these truths actually do exist in time—the first century and our own. We do not ignore doctrine to study case histories, but neither do we study doctrine in a vacuum. The chasm still exists between the first century and ours, but it is connected, not with a flimsy, treacherous tightrope, but with a massive, solid bridge, the bridge of truth and of the power of Scripture to achieve its goals in every age. It is a bridge across which we can walk and span the centuries, talking now with Peter and Paul, now with our neighbors next door. Fears, anxieties, loneliness concerned an Epaphroditus or a Euodia as much as a Brad or a Becky. Perhaps the simplest way to express this approach to application is by mentally asking two questions. These are questions that ideally should be in the minds of the congregation: "What should I have decided or done myself if I were in the biblical life-situation?" and "What should I therefore decide or do in my own situation today?"[25]

Lloyd Perry suggests analyzing biblical passages that deal with life situations with several questions in mind. How did the problem arise? Is it an economic problem? Is it sociological or physical or psychological? Does the solution we see in the biblical passage apply to a similar situation today, or is it only relevant to that situation? What steps were, and can be today, taken to solve the problem?[26]

The term "life-situation" as applied to biblical preaching has a long and varied history that need not deter us here. It is important to realize, however, that at times it has been used by those who have not acknowledged the full inspiration and authority of the Scriptures nor recognized the existence and importance of objective propositional truth in Scripture. That is, they have failed to see that the Bible contains truths about God and his world that are capable of expression in propositions of fact valid for all time. Their preaching tends to be exclusively relational, that is, centering on personal dimensions rather than subjecting all aspects of personal existence and relationships to the objective doctrines of Scripture.

There is, of course, a relational dimension to preaching. But the whole of human existence and the circumstances and needs of the individual must take their place, and indeed will only find solution, in proper relation to God's eternal truths, his works in history, and his revelation of himself and his truths in history and in Scripture.

Preach to the Inner Heart Needs as Well as to External Circumstances

We are often reminded that if we are going to change the world, we have to start by changing people. This means more than regeneration, although that is certainly basic. The average person in the pew is not usually interested in even the best of challenges (building the church, helping people, personal evangelism, or whatever), unless he or she has a sense of affirmation, self-esteem, and personal reward in doing it. Whether we put this down to original sin or to a proper human need, the typical parishioner will bring one simple question to the sermon: "What's in it for me?" Crass as that sounds (and is), unless we recognize it, the best expository sermon we can preach may bring great admiration, but will not produce action. Solid biblical content can impart important new concepts and even plans of action, but yet fail to "speak to the heart," stir the hearers to *appropriate* the new concepts and *take* the proposed action.

What makes the difference? I hasten to say that it is *not* the adoption of some sub-Christian theory of self-love. It *is* that personal concern that distinguishes the good pastor from the mere minister. It is also the conscious employment of a skill and method. I wrote earlier of taking the hearers back with me into biblical history, of helping the congregation to experience the biblical life situation, events, and moral issues before abstracting the lesson. While it is true that unless we principalize the essence of the biblical passage, our people will not be able to reproduce the lesson in their own lives, we must make sure that they have identified closely enough with the characters or issues in the text to make that principalizing their *own*.

This means that we have to move from the general to the particular, from the group to the individual, from the description to the application. If we are relating a narrative, our people must "get into the action." If we are explaining a doctrine, they must see its personal relevance. Somehow we must (even if unobtrusively) show how the appropriation of this truth or principle will bring personal benefit. We must therefore be aware of the deep personal needs of human beings. This goes a step beyond (and a whole lot deeper) than just speaking to circumstances, however large they may loom. A recently bereaved widow is not only grieving for a departed husband. She may have lost her reason for living. She may be filled with guilt or doubt or anger. She may be questioning God. She may feel that she is not a whole person now. She may have lost (even if only temporarily) her sense of personal worth and self-esteem. Fears may have already blocked her view of God—fears about her financial security, fears lest she will not be able to make decisions, fears that no one will care for her in poor health. Without minimizing the power of biblical truths about eternal life and God's love, we must recognize that the mere repetition of doctrine may not be of much help in this circumstance.

Some years ago a small book appeared that was a great help to me in personal evangelism. It was called *The Dynamic of Service*, and was written by a missionary to Japan, E. Paget Wilkes. The thrust of the contents was that the author had learned the need for an appeal to the deep concerns of Japanese people as a means of opening their hearts for the balm of the gospel. He showed how to reach out to those who had a fear of death, an uncertainty about the future, loneliness, and so forth. This was not to make the message "man-centered," but to prepare the way for the message by showing people both their need of God and God's concern for them.

Personally, I believe that even our warnings about the consequences of sin and rejection of Christ can take human needs into account. For example, the typical contemporary person who fears loneliness and estrangement may well be moved to come to Christ more strongly by the description of the fate of apostates in Jude 13, "They are . . . wandering stars, for whom the blackest darkness has been reserved forever," than by the thought of flames. This is especially so now that we have some idea of an expanding universe and the immense distance between stars, and can contemplate with horror the idea of an astronaut lost in space forever.

To clarify the idea of preaching to personal need, and to show how this bears on exposition, I would distinguish three sermonic approaches: (1) preaching objective biblical truth; (2) preaching on issues, circumstances, or problems (preaching about contemporary issues and circumstances); and (3) person-related preaching. I would describe the first as exposition proper. It may contain the seeds of application (as Scripture always does in itself), it may be sprinkled with hints of application, or it may conclude with an application, but its basic format is the explanation of a passage. The second kind of sermon addresses matters that many of the congregation are likely to be thinking about (or should be thinking about in the pastor's opinion!). A bridge is built between the life situation of the congregation and the life situation of a biblical passage. The people are encouraged to identify with people in the biblical scene and make the appropriate decision or response. The sermon may have all of the expositional qualities and even approximately the same expository form, but it begins with the description of a circumstance, problem, or issue and concludes with the resolution of this and a practical application in the lives of the hearers. The third type goes beyond the second in that it concentrates on the inner feelings of the individual, rather than on his or her circumstances. This is not different from the second type with respect to form, but it is with respect to intent. It might begin as an exposition proper or as an issue-centered sermon, but it concludes with an application to the inner state. This might be an evangelistic appeal, an exhortation to have courage, or an affirmation of God's love.

Just as the second approach will build a bridge between contemporary and biblical life situations, so the third approach establishes an empathy between the inner state and feelings of the individual hearer and those that are addressed in the biblical passage. How does this affect the exposition? The following example may help. We have already spoken of Romans 5:1–11. We can give an equally faithful exposition either by concentrating on the saving acts of God and the process of salvation, or by concentrating on the peace, joy, and hope that God's saving work can produce in our hearts. Thus the preacher's approach and intent will modify his opening, his outline, and his application, while still conveying the same expository data as in the first or second types.

What I am dealing with in these pages is not merely producing the motivation to respond to the sermon and handle one's life-situation better. It is helping the hearer to understand himself or herself, to be affirmed as the object of God's love, perhaps also to be convicted as a sinner. This is not unrelated to motivation, or to the circumstances of life, but it goes deeper, to the "heart of the matter," indeed to the human heart itself.

Someone may fear at this point that the third approach may be so person-centered that it substitutes human concerns for the glory of God. It is true that contemporary evangelism has at times either done this or given the impression that it has. But the "chief end" of relevant evangelism, and of person-related preaching, can and should still be our enjoyment and glorification of God.

Another may fear that we will tear personal application from the biblical text. Perhaps such a reader has worked through the issue of subjective versus objective preaching of biblical history, as discussed in Greidanus's *Sola Scriptura*.[27] As Greidanus shows, the danger of uncontrolled subjectivism is real. It must be avoided, but so should a retreat into mere objectivity. The truly expository sermon will combine a faithful explanation of the passage in proper balance with and relationship to its application. The answer again lies in the context of Scripture. What are the facts? What is the life situation? What are the moral, ethical, and doctrinal issues? What was the intent of the Holy Spirit and the inspired human author in producing this text? To seek a psychological, motivational, human-centered application without asking these questions is as erroneous as allegorizing, or moralizing when these are unwarranted by the text itself.

A third fear is that theology will become the servant of relational exhortation. Quite on the contrary, we would emphasize the need for doctrinal preaching and for the preaching of biblical theology. (The difference between the two is that doctrine deals with the *synthesis* of the teaching of various passages in *propositionally stated truths*, while biblical theology refers to the emphases on *various aspects* of truth given in *distinctive ways* by the various authors of Scripture.)

The clear presentation of theology, whether in the distinctive notes of Paul, in the terminology of John or Peter or Jude, or in the individual portraits of Jesus in the synoptic Gospels, is essential to all worship and action. God's people need to be helped in the construction of a network of theological truth. Without this their worship will be impoverished and their ethical decisions will need the input of others, rather than being informed by their own grasp of God's character, ways, and will. There is always a need for great doctrinal preaching. However, this should never be presented in a sterile, isolated fashion. It must lead to a deeper relationship with God, a greater awe, a more complete obedience, for all such results of preaching are ultimately to the glory of God.

Perhaps I can illustrate the matter of personal application by listing five hypothetical outlines. The subject matter will be three concepts, God as light, God as Savior, and God as a refuge.

Type One: *Description*
1. The Lord, our Light.
2. The Lord, our Salvation.
3. The Lord, our Refuge.

Type Two: *Declaration*
1. The Lord is our Light.
2. The Lord is our Salvation.
3. The Lord is our Refuge.

Type Three: *Explanation*
1. What does it mean that the Lord is our Light?
2. What does it mean that the Lord is our Salvation?
3. What does it mean that the Lord is our Refuge?

Type Four: *Exhortation*
1. Let the Lord be your Light.
2. Let the Lord be your Salvation.
3. Let the Lord be your Refuge.

Type Five: *Application*
1. How the Lord can be our daily Light in darkness.
2. How the Lord can be our Savior when we sense our guilt.
3. How the Lord can be our strong Refuge when we feel besieged.

These examples are somewhat artificial, but I have over-simplified them in order to make the contrast clear. There is an obvious progression from the mere repetition of a biblical phrase to a personal application. If we are to move from mere exposition to an expository sermon, we need to be conscious of the way to progress from text to application.

It cannot be said that any of the five examples is wrong in itself, but it should be observed that they will lead naturally to different responses on the part of the congregation. Actually none of them is expressed here in the form of an exposition of a particular passage, although the reader will think of some passages, perhaps in the Psalms, that contains these concepts. The truth contained in these concepts could be related in such a way as to facilitate a new appreciation of God issuing in worship, could help people deal with certain circumstances in their lives, and could give them a renewed sense of personal inner confidence because God is showing himself strong on their behalf.

We are now ready to discuss what we have only sketchily touched on, the actual form of the sermon. This form must serve not only the exposition, but the application of the message.

Chapter Eight

Structuring the Sermon: The Form

Expository Sermons Need Homiletical Form

Tired old jokes about three-point sermons notwithstanding, it is a rare sermon that lacks form but yet is still easy to follow. As we observed in chapter 1, there are sermons that are sincerely intended to be expository, but that merely ramble from verse to verse. They are nothing more than a formless running commentary.

The points of a sermon outline are not merely mnemonic devices, hooks on which to hang our memory. Some may feel that a Scripture passage has enough of its own memorable points to render a sermon outline unnecessary. But the outline of a sermon is also a means of (1) sifting and grouping the data of a passage to facilitate *comprehension*, (2) focusing on the aspects of that passage that the preacher finds important for *emphasis*, and (3) moving the sermon along towards its *goal*.

The first of these functions is important because the passage may be so long or complex that the congregation (especially if some do not have the text before them or are visually handicapped) cannot easily understand the inner relationships of its parts. But also the expositor may decide to reorder the sequence of items in a passage. He may do this in order to begin with some more commonly known or understood fact and work towards something that builds on that fact. He may also decide to commence with some supporting facts in the text and progress toward the implications of these. But the supporting data may in fact appear after the statements regarding their implications, and therefore require new placement and careful structuring in an outline. We have seen earlier that the parts of a passage may be reordered as long as there is no distortion, imbalance, or confusion involved in that move.

The second function of an outline, to focus on certain aspects of a passage, must be carefully controlled. If selectivity results in excluding parts of the passage that are essential to the argument or comprehension of its message, that process is invalid. It is just at this point that the intent of the preacher may be counter to the intent of the Spirit. We have seen that one reason for expository preaching is to reduce the possibility of majoring on some themes to the minimizing of others. But there are times when there is a valid message to be drawn from a passage that does not involve every part or every doctrinal point in the entire passage. The preacher has not chosen a textual sermon, because no one sentence embodies the whole point or even provides a focus for it. The thought that he finds significant for his sermon is threaded throughout the whole paragraph. The form of the sermon can help in such a case. An outline can help the congregation to follow that thread of thought, and see its significance in its proper context.

We noted that a third function of an outline is to move the sermon along toward its goal. The importance of having a goal in mind as we format the sermon is reflected in the very sequence of chapters in this book. The reader has noted that the chapter on "function" has preceded that on "form." The reason for this is the conviction that the form should serve the function, not vice versa. The application of a passage should not be an afterthought. One's process of choosing a passage and one's burden for the message should be in dynamic relation to each other, and both should determine the form. How can one build a roadway if he does not know to where it should lead? How can I structure a sermon if I do not know what response the passage demands and I seek?

Too often we think of sermonic points as static rather than dynamic. We see them merely as organizational helpers: "Now I am talking about this," "Now I am talking about that," and so on. This approach not only can kill a sermon and put an audience to sleep, but it can paralyze the Scriptures. Bible passages are not static. They move. Even the genealogies move from century to century and from one cultural environment to another! Narratives obviously have life, but so do didactic passages. They carry the reader from an assumption to a conclusion, from some truth about God and his world to its meaning for me.

The various elements of composition that we have already discussed are in themselves dynamic. Stereo buffs talk about the dynamic range of recordings. The newest (and expensive!) equipment can remarkably expand the dynamic range, so the stereophile who sits in his living room can be enthralled by a soft passage one moment and blasted out of his chair by trumpets and timpani the next. So it is with Scripture. Where there are such contrasts, let the contrast strike the congregation with all of its force.

Is there development in a passage from a commonly known truth to one that is less known? Recognition of this can help cure two common complaints about sermons: that they simply repeat what most Christians know and, at the other extreme, that they are over the heads of most of the congregation. Good homiletical structure can prevent both of those criticisms by our (1) reviewing those parts of a passage that describe generally known Christian truths, (2) making sure that even the newest visitor understands these essentials, and then (3) building carefully step by step, as a good teacher, to the eventual presentation of some new insight into the passage. In this way there is movement from the known to the unknown.

The successive points of a skillfully crafted sermon can also provide an almost visible portrait of some Bible character. Like a graphic visualization on TV or the development of a character in a novel, drama, or movie, the preacher can vividly portray the characteristics, virtues, faults, and the eventual destiny of a character. There should not only be a dynamic unfolding of the events in the biblical personage's life, but also a tantalizing stage-by-stage revelation of his or her character, motivational drives, and spiritual vitality or deficiencies, done in such a way that the congregation dare not miss the next fascinating revelation.

Skilled homileticians who may be reading this chapter will have already sensed a problem. A congregation usually remembers what they hear at the very beginning. The main impact of a sermon is often made (whether by design or not!) in the first several minutes. How can we both capture the congregation during those first few minutes of rapt attention and at the same time move toward a climax?

This problem is not unlike the one faced by a novelist or by the producer of a drama or film. A major difference, of course, is that a sermon is not designed for entertainment but to motivate. The first minutes cannot only serve to capture attention and awaken a sense of need, but, must also provide enough substantial biblical truth to point out the direction and goal of the message. A good opening will convince the congregation not only of the *relevance* but of the *value* of what they will hear if they stay tuned in. Personally, I like to hear a sermon that not only has a clear succession of points, but that gives me a hint in advance of where it is going. The driver of a car is less likely than the passengers to be bothered by turns and bumps, because he can anticipate them. So the preacher should let his audience know where he is going in advance. Some may feel this ruins the element of suspense, but even if we want our sermon to be a cliffhanger at the end, we should give the congregation some idea as to where the cliff is at the beginning. Actually, the success of some dramas lies in the way they build up a sense of the inevitable.

What I am suggesting then is that we study the text carefully before we begin to write down our points, to see what parts of the text will contribute toward the opening "statement," and what parts lend themselves, by their very nature, to a sense of progression in the sermon. If we would like our sermon to include an introduction, a climax, and to have a final impact, we will be wise to see if we can find such in the text itself.

The great probability is that these goals will be achieved simply by following the text in its biblical sequence. That should always be our first approach. There may be other texts, however, that are best expounded by spiraling around a central word, phrase, or statement, coming closer and closer to it as we pick up the various points that prepare us for understanding it and grasping its importance. The important thing is that we do not re-order the text in our sermon so drastically that the congregation cannot follow or cannot use our approach as a model for their own personal Bible study. Remember that the Holy Spirit has inspired Scripture in the form in which it exists. There is a reason why the elements of a passage stand in the sequence in which we find them.

But what if the passage I have chosen is one that does not have enough structure or a clear enough sequence from which to derive a homiletical outline? Are my only alternatives either to try communicating with my congregation through a biblical but poorly organized sermon or, on the other hand, to choose a topical outline, using the Scripture only as resource material? The latter alternative is usually not exposition, and the former is not expository preaching. A further dilemma faces the preacher who desires to relate to a particular life situation in the experience of his congregation. It may be that this situation needs more direct attention than an expository sermon usually permits. Also to select merely one passage may mean omitting others that are equally important in addressing that situation. Suppose I do want to preach a relevant topical sermon, and yet desire to expound Scriptures. Are these two goals mutually exclusive? I have often found students to be completely frustrated when they try to bring the ideals of Bible exposition, acquired in their exegetical courses, to the ideals of homiletical theory. For example, a student might see great value in adopting one of the five "Organic Forms" suggested by Henry Grady Davis in *Design for Preaching:* (1) A Subject Discussed, (2) A Thesis Supported, (3) A Message Illumined, (4) A Question Propounded, (5) A Story Told.[28] He may feel, however, that he must choose between one such of these forms and an expository mode of preaching. Nevertheless, when we bring these forms to the Scriptures, we may well find that one of them is eminently suitable as a vehicle for the exposition of the Word. It may be that a passage can be adapted in its entirety to one such form without distortion. This possibility is seen clearly by looking at Haddon W. Robinson's *Biblical Preaching.*[29] In his chapter on "The Shapes Sermons Take," he proposes, among other procedures, "An Idea to Be Explained," "A Proposition to Be Proved," "A Principle to Be Applied," and "A Subject to Be Completed" (pp. 116-23). While these may sound somewhat similar to Davis's five "Organic Forms," they have an individual character in Robinson's work, and each can help in expounding the biblical text.

Sometimes the preacher may need to reduce the amount of time spent in direct exposition, fitting a reduced exposition into a larger framework. The same procedure can be followed when preaching to a life situation. In fact, there is no reason why two or three passages could not be treated in this way. In such a case, the passages will not be expounded in detail. Instead, each will be introduced under one of the sermon points. A sentence or two would be sufficient to locate the passage in its context for the sake of the understanding of the congregation. Several verses can then be explained and applied to the point under discussion. The next passage could be introduced and handled in the same way, and so forth. This is quite different from merely using the Scripture as a source material to bolster a point. The integrity of the passage in its context is maintained. The sequence of thought in the passage, even though it be only a few verses, is kept. The Scripture is applied in accordance with its own function within a life situation of the original writer and readers.

Likewise the application of homiletical principles can help us to present a passage in a logical compelling way, whether or not the passage itself has a structure that lends itself to preaching. The explanation of sermonic process given by Lloyd M. Perry in his *Biblical Sermon Guide* is useful here.[30] Although the expository sermon as such is listed as only one of a number of variations, this does not exclude the use of the other outlines as a basic setting and structure for exposition. There are certainly several passages of Scripture that could be expounded under Perry's first example of outline variations, the "Adverbial" or "Interrogative" sermon: I. What Is Prayer? II. Who Should Pray? III. Why Should We Pray?[31] This is only the first of a number of examples that could be given from that chapter.

Three Types of Sermons

We might classify sermons into three basic types. One is *structurally expository*, that is, its structure is determined by the structure of the biblical passage. A second type is *indirectly expository*. The sermon includes exposition, but the sermon structure is not determined solely by that passage. The third type is *topical*. Its structure is not determined by a passage, although it may be informed by one or more biblical passages.

To consider these further, let us take them in reverse order. The *topical* sermon will vary considerably according to the theology, concerns, and method of the preacher. It may be very biblical, in that it conveys the essence of biblical teaching on a topic. However, its methodology is not reproducible in the personal Bible study of the congregation. There is no clear presentation of the course of argument or sequence of events of a single passage. Some expository purists spurn this kind of message as inferior. I would like to suggest that it has great value when used appropriately. However, a congregation that hears only (or even mainly) topical sermons is missing some benefits of direct Bible teaching. My earlier comments on the value of expository preaching indicate why that is so.

The sermon that is *indirectly expository* may, in some ways, be superior homiletically to many straight expositions. If, for example, one follows the propositional method of Lloyd Perry, he can apply this either to a topical or to an expository message. He can select a passage (e.g., Romans 4), establish the subject (Justification); state a theme (Justification by faith, not works); form a proposition (We are justified by faith alone); and present a transitional sentence ("Paul shows us in Romans 4 why it is only by faith that we can be cleared of guilt before God."). He can then proceed to an exposition of the passage point by point, because his homiletical framework is based on the sequence of teaching in that passage. Perry has several types of procedure, such as "modification," "clarification," and "investigation," each of which can readily be used to give form and direction to an exposition.[32] This approach is especially helpful when the preacher desires to concentrate on one theme in a passage. It can save the preacher from losing direction and power as sometimes happens when we try to treat a number of themes in a passage equally.

It must be said, however, that this or any approach other than structural exposition can allow a preacher to stray from the true main teaching of a passage if he is not careful. He may see a topic in the text that is not really a significant part of the biblical author's train of thought, and wrest it from its context even while doing lip service to that context. He would do better to find a passage that clearly taught the truth he feels led to preach on and give an exposition of that passage instead. It is also all too easy to impose on a passage an emphasis or meaning that is not there, for the sake of filling out an outline. Each point may be truth, and may be biblical truth, but if it does not grow out of a passage, the preacher may be suspected of dishonesty in claiming to find it there. Also, he will not be giving a good model of Bible study. We decry the cults for misusing Scripture, but one can distort Scripture in the pulpit simply by trying to make it fit his homiletic mold.

Indirect exposition may also allow a broader treatment of significant biblical themes than a structurally expository sermon. Suppose, for example, that I want to preach on Jesus' parables on prayer in Luke 11 and 18. I might bind these together with some other Scripture by preaching on "Why we can have the courage to pray without ceasing." I could begin with "1. Because God commanded us," choosing a few passages such as Paul's "Pray without ceasing" (1 Thessalonians 5:17, making sure I understand its meaning). Next I could present "2. Because Jesus illustrated patient prayer in two parables (Luke 11 and 18)." I might conclude with "3. Because God has given us some direct promises to encourage us," and provide a few such promises with a brief explanation of each. Such a sermon would include an exposition of the two parables in compact form. Admittedly in this case I have chosen for my illustration two of the most difficult parables to interpret! But is that not just the sort of problem we often face in our sermon preparation? In such a case we are challenged to tackle the exegetical problems and package the passage well for preaching.

If the passages are too complex to treat briefly within the confines of such a sermon, I might consider extending my sermon into a series, entitled the same: "Why we can have the courage to pray without ceasing." My individual sermons would then vary in form from each other. The first one, on the commands, will treat these individually. The second one (or two), on the parables, will be structurally expository. The final sermon(s) may take a different form. This approach will have an additional benefit: it will add variety to my preaching while still featuring exposition.

If I choose to preach on 1 Thessalonians 5:17 for my first message, I will be preaching a *textual* sermon. I have not listed this as a separate type, although it is customary to do so. For the purposes of this book I am considering it as an opportunity for *indirect exposition.* That is, the text ought not to be preached without some reference to its place in context. Either by occasional references to the context or by a treatment of it at one place in the sermon, the preacher will establish its meaning within the flow of thought. The textual sermon can be in part topical, as the preacher deals with one thought (e.g., "Why we should pray without ceasing" or "How we can pray without ceasing"). It can be in part expository, as I explain and apply the words and phrases of the text.

Some of the greatest sermons ever preached have been textual sermons. The multi-volume series edited by James Hastings in the early decades of this century, "Great Texts of the Bible" is a monument to textual preaching. A textual sermon is not in itself necessarily an expository sermon. No doubt most are not. But it can be so handled that a passage of Scripture is explained and applied and the meaning and significance of the text enriched thereby.

Structural Exposition and Its Modifications

Structural exposition should always, in my judgment, be the first method we consider, even if it may quickly give way to an indirectly expository or topical approach. By starting with a structural approach, I discipline myself to analyze the passage(s) under consideration and impress on myself their direction, main teaching(s), moral thrust, and function in their own life situation. When these matters are determined, we can begin the delicate task of restating the major points of the passage in a form that has homiletical coherence.

It is just at this point that I suggest we break from the usual concept of exposition. Structural exposition does *not* necessarily mean *linear* exposition. A brief example of this was given above in the reference to circling around a subject. Another example is seen in Haddon Robinson's distinction between inductive and deductive sermons. In the latter the basic idea appears at the beginning, with the sermon developing that idea. In the former, the inductive sermon, the congregation is led step by step to the idea. They "produce a sense of discovery in the listeners, as though they had arrived at the idea on their own."[33]

Even more variety, and indeed a variety inherent in the text itself, is possible. Let us think back to chapter 2 and the discussion of "patterns." The biblical authors do not write haphazardly nor do they waste words. If they have been led by the Spirit of God to follow a particular structural pattern or to introduce a distinctive semantic pattern, it is to catch the attention of the reader for the sake of presenting the message powerfully. It is true that the rhetoric of the first century is not the rhetoric of today. We do not usually use chiastic structure, for example. But I can either (1) observe the rhetorical structure in my study, and use conventional contemporary means to convey the message, or (2) let the congregation see the original structure (thereby contributing to their Bible knowledge), and then proceed to use it as it stands. I find that people are often fascinated by this, and feel that they are learning something most people have not discovered about the text. A good example is the chiastic structure of Luke 1:67–79, the Song of Zechariah at the birth of John the Baptist. The order of the chiasm is as follows:

```
1   "come" (v. 68)
  2   "his people" (v. 68)
    3   "salvation" (v. 69)
      4   "prophets" (v. 70)
        5   "salvation . . . enemies . . . hand" (v. 71)
          6   "fathers" (v. 72)
            7   "covenant" (v. 72)
            7'  "oath" (v. 73)
          6'  "father" (v. 73)
        5'  "rescue . . . hand . . . enemies" (v. 74)
      4'  "prophet" (v. 76)
    3'  "salvation" (v. 77)
  2'  "his people" (v. 77)
1'  "come" (v. 78)
```

This structure can certainly be pointed out during the course of the sermon. In some informal situations it could even be printed and distributed, or shown on an overhead projector. It can then be explained in terms of the Old Testament prophecies and the fulfillment in the coming of John the Baptist, forerunner of the Messiah. The essentials can be formed into a sermon of modification. For example, if this passage were preached at Christmas time, the lead-in and out-line could be as follows:

> We can praise God today, as Zechariah did, because:
> 1. God has *come* to us.
>   (Refer to the coming of Christ.)
> 2. God *saves* his *people*.
>   (Explain the gospel and how we become God's new people.)
> 3. God will keep his *promise*.
>   (Stress coming to God with confidence.)

It will be necessary to explain at each point where the key words occur in the passage, what they mean in this context, what the verses that contain them are teaching, and how all this can be applied today. It is not an easy passage, but such a treatment (1) expounds the passage in the unique form Luke wrote it, (2) allows one to preach on a passage seldom heard in the pulpit, and (3) reduces a heavy passage to a few clear points without evacuating it of its meaning. The themes can be explained in their Old Testament sense and then in their Christian application. Because the covenant/oath is at the center of the chiasm, this will naturally be the pivotal point, or the climax, of the sermon. God keeps his promise! This can easily and biblically lead into a gospel application. I have deliberately selected what may seem to be a most unlikely ancient rhetorical device to show that even this can be used in its original form!

The point we are making is obvious: any structural or semantic pattern we observe in a passage should be examined to see if it has potential for a sermon outline. But it is not enough simply to reproduce that pattern. It must be studied to see what it is accomplishing in its own context. How does the pattern move our thinking along? Where does it take us? What truths does it emphasize? Why does it emphasize them? Do the elements of the pattern answer such basic questions as "Who?" or "What?" (Perry's process of clarification) or "Why?", "How?", "When?", or "Where?" (Perry's process of modification)? Does the pattern help us to see more clearly some issue or question, some idea, some proposition or principle (to take up some of Davis's and Robinson's categories)? If so we might next see if these elements by themselves present the flow and substance of the passage. If they do, we can use them as our main stations along the way of the sermon. If not, we should determine the best way to analyze the passage, again looking at the paragraph outline, and then see if the elements of the pattern can be brought out within that general structure.

Procedure

The way we apply all the foregoing suggestions is crucial. Our analysis of the passage may be thorough and accurate, but if this is not carried over into an appropriate homiletical structure it will be as useless as a car with a perfectly functioning engine but a broken transmission. I recommend the following procedure:

1. Do the preparatory work indicated earlier: Survey the context, note the dominant characteristics and themes, and do the practical exegesis of significant elements in the passage.

2. Construct one or more tentative outlines for the expositional core of your sermon, or for those parts of it that will be expositional if the sermon is indirect exposition. Determine whether the entire passage lends itself to the burden of your sermon or whether you will need to concentrate on only one part of it. Structure your outline(s) on whichever of the following is most appropriate to (1) the literary form of the passage; (2) the significant elements of com-

position, semantic patterns, and, above all, the narrative or logical flow of the passage; (3) the function of the passage in its life setting and the application you believe is appropriate to the life situation of your congregation; (4) your own style of preaching. Keep the possible sermonic forms in mind as you proceed, ready to consider also some new sermon type if those you usually use are not appropriate. Your sermon may be structured from:

a. The *main clauses* in the passage, as determined through a paragraph (clause) analysis as described earlier, provided that the main clauses are not only so syntactically, but are also the main ideas in the author's sequence of thought.

b. A sequence of *subordinate clauses* or *phrases*, if these (1) are *foundational*, or provide such *supporting data* for the main clauses, that they call for major attention, or (2) convey the *purpose* or *result* of the main clauses so significantly that they ought to control the direction of the sermon. Beware of doing this just to emphasize favorite ideas of your own.

c. A *combination* of main and subordinate clauses and phrases, if this is the best way to capture the direction of the author's thought.

d. A *dominant truth* or *ethical imperative*, if this, rather than a linear sequence of ideas, characterizes the passage (e.g., 1 Corinthians 13; Hebrews 11).

e. A *structural pattern* other than normal clause sequence, or a *semantic pattern* (see chapter 2), if such conveys a major emphasis of the author and is not merely stylistic.

f. A *narrative structure*, based on sequence of events or an unfolding character delineation.

3. Keep in mind the following as you structure the main outline and subpoints:

a. Your single-sentence summary of the passage.

b. Key ideas. From key words and phrases, main clauses, terms in the same semantic field, logical elements of composition, and other "patterns" and linguistic phenomena.

c. Supporting data. Information, usually in subordinate constructions, that provides foundational doctrine or assumptions, motives, goals or objectives, means, modes, etc.

d. Emotional "color." Moods (e.g., joy, anger, confidence, boasting, sadness, fear), which may be an essential part of the communication.

e. Trajectories in the context and book as a whole. Themes,

moods, doctrines, imperatives, etc., that move through the passage in hand and that cannot be treated in isolation from the larger context.

4. Test your outline to be sure it is:

a. Faithful to the text, conveying the main truths or imperatives in the same balance they have in the text. If you have written a one-sentence summary of the passage, as proposed earlier, does your outline accord with its essence?

b. Obvious from the text, and, in particular, discernible in the English translation that most of the congregation have before them.

c. Relevant to the hearers and goal oriented, leading the congregation to the conclusion and application that ought to be drawn from the passage.

d. Neither trite nor static, but dynamic, stimulating interest and response. It should move toward a climax.

Examples

We are now ready to work out a sermon outline, drawing together the ideals and approaches we have mentioned so far. I would like to show how one passage, Romans 5:1–11, can be structured into two different sermons, each of which is faithful to the text, yet applies it in a distinctive way.

Sermon Number One

First of all we may follow a basic paragraph (clause) analysis to determine the *main clauses*. An example was given in chapter 3 (pp. 55f.). The following is a slight modification of that analysis, reproduced here for convenience.

v. 1   Therefore,
            Since we have been justified through faith,
      we have peace with God
            through our Lord Jesus Christ,
v. 2   through whom we have . . . access
               by faith
               into this grace
                  in which we now stand.
      And we rejoice in the hope of the glory of God.
v. 3   Not only [is this] so,
      but we rejoice also in our sufferings,
            because we know that

suffering produces perseverance,
perseverance [produces] character,
and character [produces] hope.
v. 5 And hope does not disappoint us,
because God has poured out his love
into our hearts
by the Holy Spirit,
whom He has given us.
v. 6 . . . at just the right time
when we were still powerless,
Christ died for the ungodly.
v. 7 One rarely dies for a righteous person
One may . . . dare to die for a good person
v. 8 But God demonstrates his love for us in this:
While we were yet sinners
Christ died for us.
v. 9 Since we have now been justified
by his blood,
how much more
shall we be saved from God's wrath
through him.
v. 10 For if we were reconciled to him
by the death of his Son
when we were enemies
having been reconciled
how much more
shall we be saved
through his life.
v. 11 Not only (is this) so,
but we also rejoice in God
through our Lord Jesus Christ
through whom we have now received reconciliation.

There are four main clauses in verses 1 through 5. These represent four basic affirmations of Paul. They are so clear an expression of Paul's sequence of thought that they will yield an excellent outline.

We have peace with God (v. 1).
We rejoice in the hope of the glory of God (v. 2).
We also rejoice in our sufferings (v. 3).
Hope does not disappoint us (v. 5).

These main clauses are not only sufficient to give us a basic sermon outline, but they are comprehensive enough to allow us to include the rest of the entire paragraph as vital supporting information.

From these clauses we can structure an outline that varies very little from the wording of the passage itself. If my one-sentence summary of the passage is: "Justification through faith in Christ results in a life of peace and confidence," and if I follow somewhat Perry's process of modification, or Robinson's "idea to be explained," I might come up with the following:

Being made right with God through Christ results in a life of peace and confidence such as many people long to have.

1. We have peace with God.
2. We have joy because our hope is centered on God's glory.
3. We can even have joy in sufferings.
4. We will never be disappointed by a lost hope.

It will be seen that in the preceding I have begun to modify the biblical language slightly in order to begin a transition to contemporary idiom and circumstances. The outline is faithful to the text, clearly discernible from any English translation, consistent with the function and goal of the passage, and dynamic. That is, it moves from a statement about our present relationship with God (peace) to a promise of the future (hope), then to a universal experience (suffering), and finally to the resolution of a common fear (disappointed hope). It moves from theology to application.

Now that I have a tentative basic outline, I proceed to a further study of the text for *key ideas* that must be included if I am to give a faithful exposition. By laying out the passage as we did in the analysis above, we can easily identify words that are repeated, linked by their occurrence in a pattern of syntax, or semantically related. First of all I notice that the word, "rejoice," occurs in verses 2–3, and 11. This mood of joy must be strongly present in my presentation. I observe that there are several initial significant prepositional phrases: "with God" (v. 1), "through our Lord Jesus Christ" (v. 1), and "through whom" (v. 2). These have a close equivalent in verse 11: "in God," "through our Lord Jesus Christ," "through whom." Such phrases lead me to the observation that any presentation of this passage must show that the blessings of justification are received only in close association with God. Other phrases in the passage also bring this out, for example, verse 5, "by the Holy Spirit." Words having to do with life and death (including the word "blood" in verse 9) appear frequently in verses 6 through 10. Words that describe the person before the Christian experience are also striking: "powerless" (v. 6), "ungodly" (v. 6), "sinners" (v. 8), and "enemies" (v. 10). The double occurrence of the words "suffering," "perseverance," "character," and "hope" (vv. 3–5) draws attention to the sequence of thought there.

All this information also shows me what the *supporting data* are for the main affirmations of verses 1 through 5. The clause analysis also helps to see exactly what truths support the main affirmations. For example, the fourth point ("We will never be disappointed by a lost hope") is supported by the fact that "God poured out his love into our hearts by the Holy Spirit" (v. 5). This in turn is supported by the fact that Christ died for us, not because we were lovable, but even when we were hostile (vv. 6–8). This gives confidence to our hope. Further, verses 9 and 10 provide additional support by showing that what God has done for us in the past is so great that we can know without doubt what he will do in the future. The affirmations of verses 1 through 5 in this way receive support by the rest of the passage. Verse 11 provides a further statement and a recapitulation in words similar to verse 1.

Having established a legitimate sequence of thought based on the grammar of the passage, and having determined what other facts and supporting data need to be included, our next step is to consider the *emotional "color"* of this text. Is there any dominant emotion observable in the writer or that the writer obviously desires to produce in the reader? In this case the writer's feelings come through strongly and almost dominate the entire passage. The air of *confidence* that characterizes these verses must not be lost to the sermon. Paul wants his readers to recognize the benefits of justification, be strengthened in confidence through that recognition, and lift their hearts toward God in response (note v. 11).

My next step is to see what *trajectories* are discernible in the passage. By that I mean those themes, moods, doctrines, imperatives, and such that not only are present in the passage itself, but that move through the larger context that precedes and follows the passage, and even perhaps through the entire book. One such is the idea of justification through faith. Another is the meaning of the death of Christ. There are others, including suffering and hope, that are picked up again in chapter 8. It is especially important to observe such trajectories if we are preaching through the entire book. If this is indeed part of such an expository series, each of these major themes should be expanded at some point in the series.

When that is the case, the treatment of that theme might need to take a proportionately larger place in the sermon than its occurrence in the passage at hand might otherwise warrant. Such temporary disproportion will, however, be balanced out over the course of the entire series.

In the sermon as outlined above, each of the four points will need to be applied specifically to the life of the individual hearer. Each item, "peace," "hope," and so on, will need to be explained, illustrated, and linked with daily life. In this way the function of the passage in its original setting will become its function in the life situation of the congregation.

Sermon Number Two

The preceding illustrates the most natural way to preach from Romans 5:1–11. However, the entire procedure can actually be reversed. Suppose we take as our starting point not the main clauses, but the supporting data in verses 6 through 10, working logically from cause to effect. I might choose this "reverse" outline if my message is intended for an audience that may not have an evangelical or strong doctrinal background. It would be appropriate for a gospel message. In this case the essential content and even the type of sermon process could be the same as in the previous example. My outline could be as follows:

> How can I have a peace, joy, and hope that will transcend suffering and human uncertainty?
> 1. Recognize the state we are in apart from Christ.
>   a. Powerless (v. 6)
>   b. Ungodly (v. 6)
>   c. Sinners (v. 8)
>   d. Enemies (v. 10)
> 2. Acknowledge what God has done for us.
>   a. His Son died for us (v. 10)
>   b. His Son lives for us (v. 10)
> 3. Receive the love God expressed in the death of Christ (v. 8) and offered through the Holy Spirit (v. 5).
> 4. Believe in the Lord and thereby be "justified" (v. 1) and "reconciled" (v. 11).
> 5. Rest in God's peace and enjoy him (vv. 1–5, 11)

It will not be necessary to go into the same detail as we did in analyzing the first sermon. The appropriateness of this outline should already be clear. Both of the sample sermons on Romans 5 would be expository. Both are based on the elements found in the text and on their logical relationship to each other.

Examples From Matthew 6

Both of the preceding outlines were based on an analysis of clauses and phrases, with only a secondary use of verbal patterns. The following examples are based *primarily* on such patterns.

Matthew 6:1–18 moves from the general to the particular. A generalization is stated at the outset: "Be careful not to do your 'acts of righteousness' before men, to be seen by them." The particulars are introduced by the repeated phrase, "When you . . . ," that is, "When you give" (v. 2), "When you pray" (v. 5), and "When you fast" (v. 16).

Nevertheless, I would *not* suggest using these three as the main points without some alteration. The reason is twofold. First, Jesus' three examples given are not typical of today. People in our culture today do not make a show of giving, praying, and fasting in the same manner as in Jesus' day. Second, in the passage itself, the section on prayer includes the Lord's Prayer, which far outweighs the examples and teachings in the other sections. Therefore I would suggest one of the following: (1) Using the three ancient examples as introductory to a sermon containing examples relevant to contemporary life. The sermon theme could be, "Religion on show, then and now." The three examples of Matthew 6 could constitute the first sermon point; with modern examples following in the other points. (2) Using the three examples in Matthew as the introduction to each part of the sermon, but using contemporary headings. For example, the theme could be "Religion isn't for show." The main headings could be "showing off your generosity" (from "When you give"), "showing off your piety" (from "When you pray"), and "showing off your self-discipline" (from "When you fast"). (3) Using the three examples in Matthew to provide the biblical setting for a sermon on the Lord's Prayer.

The next major section in Matthew 6 begins with a prohibition, "Do not store up for yourselves treasures on earth" (v.19). This is the first of three prohibitions. The others are, "Do not worry" (v.25) and "Do not judge" (7:1). These, in turn, are followed by three positive commands, the first of which is itself a triple command: "Ask, seek, knock" (v.7), "Enter" (v.13), and "Watch out" (v.15).

This pattern is more obvious in Greek (because of similar grammatical forms) but can easily be pointed out in English. Such patterns help us to preach on the Sermon on the Mount, which is rather difficult to outline for today's audience.

Still another way to structure a sermon from the Sermon on the Mount by observing patterns is to note the three references in the Sermon to pagans, "Do not even pagans do that?" (5:47), "Do not keep on babbling like pagans" (6:7), and "For the pagans run after all these things" (6:32). The first has to do with relationships with other people, the second with relationship to God (in prayer), and the third with relationship to material possessions. A good part of the Sermon on the Mount can be taught under these three subjects, perhaps under the title "How to Live Like a Pagan."

Chapter Nine

Preaching From
Difficult Texts

A glance at the topics covered in this section will show that texts may be "difficult" for different reasons. Although I have not categorized them, they could be grouped roughly under several headings. Some are difficult because of their literary form. Parables and proverbial sayings, for example, are quite different from straightforward narrative or propositional statements. In the case of parables, we need to work with extreme care, so that we analyze them appropriately without allowing their vital message to expire in the process of dismemberment. Other texts that are more straightforward are also difficult to preach from because their interpretation is uncertain.

A totally different kind of difficulty exists when the passage itself is very clear, but touches on sensitive or controversial issues. We might say that the problem here is not in the text but in the way the congregation might react to it. Here the preacher's qualities of good judgment, empathetic understanding, and love are as important as exegetical skill.

Still another category includes texts that may be relatively clear to the exegete and whose message will be readily accepted by the congregation, but that have inherent complexities that make explanation difficult. I would include here those texts that may involve critical issues. In such cases the preacher has to decide how much technical information should be brought into the sermon. The greater the preacher's scholarly ability the more conscientious he will probably be in wanting to include all the relevant data. There are times, however, when simplicity is a greater virtue than comprehensiveness. I once went to hear a well-known Bible conference speaker to see what I could learn about his preaching style. To put it another way (and to be painfully honest), I wanted to see why he was invited to speak at many more conferences than

I was! I was appalled to hear him give one interpretation of a passage without so much as hinting that there was another common (and perhaps more valid) interpretation of the passage. What I learned was that conference audiences, and probably most congregations, want to hear a clear, uncomplicated exposition that leaves them confident that they understand the passage and its application. The same sermon preached to a seminary or knowledgeable university student audience would have been a failure and would probably have brought the preacher into disrepute. I will suggest below a "better way" to handle complex and controversial passages.

It is basic not only to the consideration of "difficult" passages, but also to hermeneutics and the preparation of sermons in general that we recognize differences of *genre* in the Bible. The interpretation of a passage must be consistent with the nature of the literature under consideration. Parable, apocalypse, and poetry (to name three obvious examples) have certain characteristics inherent to their genre. The study of genre lies outside the scope of this book, but is certainly preliminary to homiletics. I would suggest reading "The Genre of New Testament Literature and Biblical Hermeneutics" by Gordon Fee in *Interpreting the Word of God,* edited by S. J. Schultz and M. A. Inch.[34]

Parables

The very strength of a parable, its appeal to the familiar, is a problem when transferring the story from one culture to another. The preacher who knows the culture of first-century Palestine should be in the best position to preach from the parables. However the converse may be true if he forgets that his congregation does not share his familiarity with the background. If the congregation remains in the dark in this respect, what should be a journey from the "unknown to the known" becomes a groping in the darkness. Also the clarity and "punch" that the original hearers perceived and felt in the parable is often lost as we struggle to determine what its real point is.

The preacher may be pardoned if he finds recent studies on the parables confusing. If he has read some of the better known works on parables written in the nineteenth century or based on nineteenth-century literature, he will be familiar with what is known as the "allegorizing" approach to the parables. He will think that the spiritual way to preach a parable is to find a spiritual meaning in each character, element, or turn of event. If one's knowledge of parabolic interpretation was gained from writers who followed Jülicher's reaction against allegorization, he will try to find just one main point in each parable. It may come as a surprise to him that more recent study of the parables sees them as art forms, with many points of correspondence to life. This is not the same as allegorization, in that it seeks to understand the story in all of the vivid color and with all of the mental associations that the original reader had in mind, without trying to draw a spiritual lesson from each point. Those who have learned to interpret the parables existentially will shy away from critical analysis and seek to allow the parable to speak to the hearer in terms of his or her circumstances and understanding. Preachers who have been able to keep up with the most recent approaches to the parables will be familiar with structuralism and its attempt to interpret the parables in terms of actants and with regard to overarching ideas and values. Those who are conscious of the "two horizons" of Gadamer and others will be very conscious of the difficulty with which anyone in a culture as far removed from the first century as ours is has in understanding the world of customs, thought, and values within which Jesus' audiences heard and understood his parables.

To illustrate the problem we have in approaching a first-century Jewish parable, we may consider Jesus' simple story about the Pharisee and the publican. We have been conditioned to think of Pharisees as proud hypocrites. Similarly, we have read in the Gospels of our Lord's kindness to repentant publicans, and therefore tend ourselves to have a certain sympathy for them. Even before we read the words of the Pharisee's prayer, we are conditioned to interpret this negatively. We then listen to the penitential prayer of the publican approvingly. But Jesus' first-century Palestinian audience would have heard the two prayers differently. To them, while some Pharisees were indeed known for their pride and hypocrisy, the Pharisees were highly respected as those who maintained a high standard of piety and fidelity to God's law. Publicans, on the other hand, were despised as greedy, shrewd, and compromisers with Rome. The rejection of the first and acceptance of the second would have come as a surprise to the original hearers of the story.

It is obvious that the more we know of the cultural background of the parables the better able we will be to relate to them appropriately to a modern congregation. In addition to this, the basic principles of hermeneutics that we learned in seminary must be applied carefully to the parable. The context must be observed. What circumstances or dialogue precede the parable? Is there some topic or some point that Jesus is seeking to make with which the parable must be connected if it is to be understood in context? What comments of Jesus or of the author of the Gospel follow? Does the concluding application make the meaning of the parable clear? Within the story itself is there some striking climax? That is, is there something that is so obvious that it would naturally draw the attention of the original hearer? It is the nature of yeast universally to affect the entire batch of dough. Therefore, in the parable of the leaven, there is no question as to what the dominant idea is. The interpretive problem is whether the pervasive leaven is to be understood as good or evil in nature. In contrast there are times when the original hearer would have his attention caught by something that is totally unexpected or out of place. The reaction of the older brother in the story of the prodigal son is an example of this. To put it another way, we need to find out where the impact of the parable was.

When we have done all of this, we need to remember that the force of Jesus' parables lies in drawing the hearer into the story itself, making an ethical or moral decision about the circumstances, and then being led to apply that decision to him or herself. Just as David reacted in righteous indignation against the man who stole the poor man's sheep, only to be told by the prophet Nathan, "You are the man!" so we are drawn into the story and find ourselves "caught" by it. The challenge to the preacher is to draw the congregation into the life situation of the parable so completely that they will identify with the ethical or moral issues involved, make a decision with respect to them, and then apply that decision appropriately in their own lives.[35]

Other Figures of Speech

Because most figures of speech are brief and probably would not constitute an entire expositional sermon as would a parable, we need not go into much detail here. In order to interpret such figures accurately, it is advisable to consult a book on hermeneutics that deals with them. Such a treatment will be found in *Interpreting the Bible* by A. Berkeley Mickelsen.[36] It would be good to review such a section occasionally so as to keep oneself alert for the recognition of figures that may unexpectedly appear in the text before us. In addition to that, it would be good to consult the Index of Scriptures at the end of Mickelsen's work whenever preparing a sermon, to be sure that any issues regarding figures of speech or other items for that matter, are recognized. Also exegetical commentaries should be consulted as an aid in recognizing and interpreting figures of speech. Commentaries sometimes use the technical names of figures of speech without explanation. Therefore, it is good to have such a work as Richard Soulen's *Handbook of Biblical Criticism* for an explanation of these and other literary terms.[37]

Narratives

It may seem that narratives are not "difficult" and therefore have no place in this section. It is true that in comparison with parables they are straightforward. However there are certain difficulties that may be even more serious because they are not obvious. Consider the following possibilities: (1) the congregation may be unfamiliar with the larger context, (2) the congregation may be unfamiliar with the setting (cultural, historical, geographical, etc.), (3) the narrative may be hard to follow, (4) the narrative may have a miraculous element (see that topic below), (5) the narrative may not seem to have a "moral" and be hard to apply in a sermon, (6) it may be hard to know what is normative and what is nonnormative, a problem especially in the Book of Acts, (7) in the Gospels there may be problems of alleged discrepancies between the Synoptics (see pages 151-54).

To name such difficulties is in itself enough to stimulate our attention to them. If, for example, we keep in mind that the congregation may be unfamiliar with the larger context, we will be careful to determine how much of the preceding context needs to be explained or, if in a series, repeated. As regards the background of narratives, we have already discussed the importance of helping the congregation to imagine themselves in the life setting of the story. Careful attention to discourse structure as already described will help guide the congregation through the narrative. Other more specific issues will be discussed below.[38]

Miracle Stories

The difficulty with miracle stories lies in two areas: apologetics and application. It is not within our scope here to discuss the philosophical or scientific aspect of the miraculous. What is important for us is that we have the wisdom to know when to introduce such issues into the sermon. Some apologetic defense of the miracle stories is useful for any congregation. This is true, of course, especially for young people and college students. Too much of an emphasis, however, can not only detract from the goal of the sermon, but also cause the congregation to dwell too much on the problems. This can awaken doubts which were not previously troubling the hearer.

The matter of application should be of even greater concern to the preacher. I see two related problems here. One is that he may misunderstand the purpose for which Jesus performed miracles and for their continuance in the Book of Acts. The second is the spiritual significance that we attach to the miracles today. It was long assumed that the miracles were basically evidential in nature. The fact that the Gospel of John features a series of "signs" or miracles pointing to the divine Sonship of Christ has perhaps led many to assume that the miracles in the synoptic Gospels always served the same purpose. It is true that the identity and authority of Jesus were affirmed by his miracles. Jesus said this clearly in Mark 2:10–11, " 'But that you may know that the Son of Man has authority on earth to forgive sins. . . .' He said to the paralytic, 'I tell you, get up, take your mat and go home.' "

But Jesus performed miracles for other reasons as well. The Gospels make it clear that Jesus' miracles of healing and feeding (cf. the narratives of the feeding of the five thousand) were acts of compassion. Jesus' miracles were also expressions of the power of the kingdom. He told the Pharisees, when he drove out demons by the Spirit of God, "The kingdom of God has come upon you" (Matthew 12:28). This kind of miracle was part of Jesus' continuing war against Satan and his forces. When the seventy-two disciples returned from their mission with the report, "Lord, even the demons submit to us in your name," Jesus replied, "I saw Satan fall like lightning from heaven" (Luke 10:17–18). Presumably the miracles performed in the Book of Acts were for the same purposes as those performed by Jesus. One aspect of these is emphasized by the author of Hebrews: "God also testified to it by signs, wonders and various miracles, and gifts of the Holy Spirit distributed according to his will" (Hebrews 2:4).

Therefore the expositor who preaches on a miracle story must be sure that both he and his congregation understand the purpose for which the particular miracles under consideration were performed. There may be more than one purpose involved, of course, but usually one is predominant. The goal of the sermon should be related to the function of the miracle in the passage being preached.

The second difficulty that miracle stories entail lies in the tendency of many preachers to "allegorize" or "spiritualize" the miracles. In this case as with the preceding, we must begin with a reference to the Gospel of John. In this Gospel the miracles do tend to have symbolic meaning. This is especially clear with respect to the healing of the blind man in John 9. In this case John has a concluding dialogue between Jesus and the Pharisees about spiritual blindness that makes this unmistakably clear. However this does not give the preacher license to "spiritualize" all healing miracles. It is strange that a preacher who defends the historicity of the Bible and criticizes those who believe they can find truth in the Scriptures even though they consider the historical aspect erroneous and of less importance, may himself try to apply a miracle story spiritually while totally ignoring its historical context, function, and purpose. The same unhappy paradox is often found in those who stress typology. The cure for this malady is the same as that discussed just above. Observe the historical context; the sequence of thought, dialogue, and action; and the sentences that immediately follow the miracle. We may look at Mark 4:35–41 for an example. This is the miracle of the calming of the storm. While it is true that Jesus can also calm the storms of our lives, such an application taken alone reduces the force of the historical fact that Jesus actually stopped the ferocious forces of nature. It would also ignore the climax of the story that is found not in the miracle but in the response of the disciples: "They were terrified and asked each other 'Who is this? Even the wind and the waves obey him!' " The point of the story is to focus attention on the supernatural power of Jesus and ultimately on the question of his identity. It is sobering to think that a preacher who would defend to the death the doctrine of the deity of Christ might fail to give that doctrine its proper place in this parable. But concentrating on a supposedly spiritual application to the storms of our lives could result in a consequent reduction of the powerful christological message it contains.

Obscure Passages

If we were to discuss obscure passages in detail, this book would turn into a commentary. We shall limit our consideration to some procedures for handling such texts. Certainly it is basic that we use recent good exegetical commentaries and follow sound principles of hermeneutics. The preacher who has access to *New Testament Abstracts* and to some of the journals to which it refers, will be able to learn recent approaches to such texts. Passages may be obscure for one or more reasons. There may be words that appear infrequently, or only once, in the New Testament. Perhaps they are rarely found in other literature as well. There may be grammatical difficulties. Some verses do not seem to flow naturally from the preceding context. In all such cases, the preacher will need to "do his homework" before he ventures into the pulpit to offer an interpretation that may affect the lives of several hundred people.

When he finds that even after study the meaning is still obscure to him, or when he finds that there are several different interpretations of the text, he faces yet another problem. Should he explain his dilemma to the congregation? Personally, I think he should in most cases, but with much care. If a congregation is frequently told that the meaning of a text is unclear, it can shake their confidence in the Scriptures, or, at the very least, in their own ability to understand the Bible. The preacher may think he has done a fine job of exegesis and exposition, and may even increase his stature as an authority on the Bible, but he will have ruined his attempt to encourage the congregation in their own study of the Word.

In my judgment the best way to handle obscure passages is, first, to decide whether the obscurity is apparent enough to the congregation, or serious enough with respect to the interpretation of the whole passage, to require acknowledgement in the sermon. Second, if it is, I would suggest making a brief explanation as to why it is obscure. For example, the preacher could merely say that differences in culture or language, or perhaps the rarity of a word, have made it difficult for us in our culture and in our century to understand it perfectly. He should do this in such a way as to avoid any implication that the Bible is hard to understand, showing that, if we had all the information of the original hearers, we would probably have no difficulty. Third, he should select the most likely meaning, as he understands it, and present that, rather than offering two or three options equally. He should be honest in acknowledging other interpretations, but will probably help the congregation most if he decides on one and gives the entire passage coherence. Fourth, he should probably not take the congregation through the process of exegesis, unless it would be a very clear and useful model of Bible study. On the whole, the more simple his presentation, the better.

Passages With Textual Difficulties

My suggestions for obscure passages apply in almost every detail to passages that are textually uncertain. However, there is an even greater danger here. A person who learns that his Bible may not accurately convey what the original writer wrote may stumble seriously in his faith in the Scriptures. Even though the preacher may have once explained how errors have crept into copies and how the integrity of the originals is unaffected, there is always the possibility that someone now hearing his sermon did not hear the previous explanation.

Unless the Bible used by those in the congregation has a different reading from that used by the preacher, or has a footnote indicating that there is a textual variant, it is probably best not to mention the uncertainty. If it seems necessary to introduce the matter, I would encourage that the preacher affirm every time this happens, that this does not affect the integrity of the original and that no doctrine would be left unsupported if a favorite reading must be abandoned because of a more valid variant. This does not mean, as one sometimes hears, that no doctrine is affected by textual variants. That would not be true. Rather, any doctrinal statements in the Scriptures that are affected by textual variants are adequately supported by other passages.

A special situation exists for the preacher who is convinced that the efforts of most textual scholars over the past decades are valid over against the claims being made for the so-called majority text and the King James Version, but whose congregation take the other viewpoint and use only the King James Version. Their sincere concern should be acknowledged and respected. Much light can be thrown on the issue by reading *The King James Version Debate* by D. A. Carson.[39] This controversy, like others, should be kept out of the pulpit as much as possible for the sake of unbelievers and new believers who may be caused to stumble. Perhaps some teaching can be given in a less public situation, such as a Sunday school class.

Proverbial Sayings

Like figures of speech, proverbial sayings must be first recognized before they can be interpreted. A knowledge of hermeneutics and the use of a good exegetical commentary is important here. In addition, we must recognize that a proverb may be quoted in Scripture as an illustration, without the implication that it is to be taken as universal truth. We all know that proverbs can be used to contradict each other. "Absence makes the heart grow fonder" may seem to be contradicted by "Out of sight, out of mind." Nevertheless we also know that there is an element of truth in each. They are to be used as illustrations, but not absolutely. When Jesus says, "whoever is not against us is for us" (Mark 9:40), he is not stating a universal truth. He is speaking about those who were serving him but were not actually in the group of disciples. We see this from the context of Mark 9:38–41. Therefore there is no contradiction between this and Luke 11:23, "He who is not with me is against me." In that context Jesus is involved in the so-called Beelzebub controversy. The sides are drawn, and each person needs to make a decision for or against Christ.

The appearance of a proverb in a biblical passage should not be thought of so much as a problem as an opportunity to help the congregation exercise common sense in biblical interpretation. They may not have the resources in commentaries and other textbooks that the preacher has, but they can learn something valuable for their own Bible study.

Culturally Related Texts

In some ways this is the most difficult kind of passage from which to preach. Hermeneutically, we need to be careful lest we either carry over as absolute those cultural aspects that are part of a setting irrelevant to contemporary life or, on the other hand, abandon part of the essential message in the attempt to make a cultural transition. Pastorally, we may find our congregation unable to understand or accept the fact that certain adjustments need to be made in the application of Scripture from culture to culture. This is particularly difficult when a church follows certain beliefs or practices as part of its heritage that are closely tied to the culture of the New Testament world. Even to mention such matters as foot washing and male-female roles tends to produce almost involuntary reactions on the part of those for whom these are important.

Cultural relevance is not just a problem, but a matter significant for the Christian. The matter is that Christian doctrine never has been, nor should be, totally detached from human life. If we are correct in affirming that Christianity touches all areas of life, we should expect that this was true in its earliest expression in the first century. The difficulty comes when, as in the case of some Siamese twins, we need to decide the point where a safe and legitimate separation can be made. Further, when a practice is connected by the biblical author with both cultural and theological facts, the difficulty increases.

A typical passage of this nature is 1 Corinthians 11:3–16. The statement in verse 3 that "the head of every man is Christ, and the head of the woman is man, and the head of Christ is God," is clearly theological, but also requires a clear understanding of the meaning that the word "head" had for Paul and for the residents of Corinth in the first century. As I write, New Testament scholars are still examining the use of that word in Greek to find an answer. When Paul speaks about a woman whose head is "uncovered" (v.5) and ways that she "dishonors" her head just as though her head were "shaved," to what practices does he refer? Is he speaking of the hair being bound up (in contrast to hanging loose as a prostitute would have it) or is he referring to some other covering in addition to the hair? How does this relate to the idea of "dishonor"? When he speaks of the head being "shaved" does he refer to the shameful symbol of adultery? Why does Paul concentrate on the concept of shame? He goes on to speak of "disgrace" in verse 6 and in verse 14. Obviously societal concepts of the role and appearance of women are an inherent part of this passage. At the same time Paul goes on to use such theological terms as "the image and glory of

God" (v.7). The passage is complex, and it is only a dogmatic approach that would veil this fact from a congregation.

The pastoral issues are also difficult, in similar proportion to the hermeneutical ones. One problem comes with the tendency on the part of Christians to feel that when we say that the Bible is culturally *relevant,* we are implying that it is also culturally *relative.* Or, that to speak of cultural relativity implies that the Bible changes with the culture. What we need to affirm is that the Bible remains constant in its truth, but that culture changes. There is a theological truth in 1 Corinthians 11 that is constant, but attitudes to women and the cultural significance of the clothing and personal appearance of women change. A woman's hairdo does not have the significance today that it did several decades ago when bobbed hair was first introduced, let alone what it did in the first century in Corinth. Hat fashions change, and may or may not have cultural significance today. The one thing they do *not* signify is female submission. But this does not mean that head coverings are unimportant in 1 Corinthians 11. On the contrary, we must diligently seek to understand that significance and to find an appropriate expression today that will convey the theological truth of that passage. All of this needs to be done with sensitivity to the conscience of the congregation and in obedience to the revealed Word of God.

Controversial Passages

Several of the types of passages that we are considering in this chapter are controversial. This is the case with some of the obscure passages and those that are culturally related especially. But a passage may be uncertain in meaning without being controversial. By controversial, I mean susceptible to contrary interpretations, each of which is championed by a segment of the Christian church. One obvious example is Hebrews 6:1–8, along with Hebrews 10:26–31. The teaching here can be understood to support the Arminian position, which understanding is opposed by those who favor the Calvinistic doctrine of the perseverance of the saints. Unless an entire congregation is in the Reformed, or in the Wesleyan, tradition, there are likely to be some hearers who will be unhappy with the preacher's interpretation. Among other examples of controversial passages, we could cite verses in Acts 2 and 1 Corinthians 14 about tongues, Romans 9–11 on the sovereignty of God, 1 Thessalonians 4:13–5:11 and 2 Thessalonians 2:1–4 regarding the rapture and the tribulation, and Revelation 20:1–10 on the millennium. This is not the place for an interpretation of such passages (I would alienate half of my readers!), but a few words as to how to handle such texts may be helpful. In brief, we should aim at "clarity with charity." The passage can be explained clearly and consistently in accordance with the preacher's own understanding and tradition. Alternate interpretations of parts or of the whole can certainly be offered with an acknowledgement that many devout Bible-believing Christians hold a different position. The charity with which the preacher treats the alternate interpretation can have a positive effect in demonstrating the unity of the body of Christ. In doing this he may well draw rather than alienate any non-Christians who may be listening. Everyone knows that the Christian church has held varying viewpoints on such matters as baptism and the Lord's Supper for centuries. There is no reason why people should not be exposed to differing viewpoints on eschatology, soteriology, and the charismatic gifts.

A situation that is, for better or for worse, increasing these days is that students are graduating from some of the evangelical but doctrinally pluralistic seminaries with minds still open concerning some of the controversial issues and the relevant texts. Insofar as this represents a desire to be faithful to the text rather than merely to a tradition, this is commendable. However, if it stems from indecisiveness or shallow exegesis, it is dangerous. There is one commitment, however, that all preachers, whether dogmatic, undecided, or in between, can make, that is to the *function* of the texts in question. Hebrews 6 has certain injunctions that can be preached with fervor and that can bring conviction regarding false profession and wavering under trial whether or not the preacher has his doctrine straight. First Thessalonians 4 can bring comfort to pre-, post-, and mid-tribulationists. First Thessalonians 5 can warn the unbeliever of wrath to come, whatever the preacher's eschatology may be. This is not to say that differences can be glossed over, or that they should be. However, the preacher who considers the whole context and the purpose of the passage in its life setting will be able to preach the passage in the power of the Holy Spirit so that it can accomplish its God-given purpose even among those who may differ with certain aspects of his interpretation.

Typology

This is more of a problem in the exposition of the Old Testament than of the New Testament. The preacher of the Old Testament will need a basic understanding of hermeneutics and of the various approaches to typology. He will need to decide whether to hold rigorously to the principle of not interpreting any passage typologically that is not so interpreted in the New Testament, or whether to adopt a more flexible approach. The expositor of the New Testament has a different problem. He will need to interpret specific passages that refer back to the Old Testament. By their very appearance in the New Testament they do establish a correspondence with some Old Testament person, thing, or event. Several passages immediately come to mind: Matthew 12:39–41 about Jonah, 1 Corinthians 10:1–4 about the Passover, and 1 Peter 3:20, 21 about baptism and Noah's ark. A special problem exists in Matthew in those places where he seems to be using quotations from the Old Testament in a way that gives them a completely different meaning from what they had in their original context. One example is Matthew 2:15, "and so was fulfilled what the Lord had said through the prophets: 'Out of Egypt I called my son.'" The interpretation of this text, which applies to the baby Jesus what was originally said about the people of Israel, should be consistent with the expressed intent of both the original passage and its context in Matthew. In this case, further study will show that Matthew is referring back, not to the historical event itself, but to the commentary on it by the prophet Hosea. Israel was God's "son" in a corporate sense, and Jesus was God's unique eternal Son. This verse is part of a larger pattern in Matthew, in which Matthew is showing a number of parallels between the experience of Israel and the experience of Jesus. Whether or not one labels this typology, the principle that must govern the interpreter is the same: the integrity of the contextual meaning in the Old Testament, as well as that in the New, must be maintained. Interpretations of the New Testament that tear away Old Testament passages from their historical context, thereby ignoring the progress of God's truth and work in the Old Testament context, are in error, no matter how "spiritual" they may seem.

Multiple Levels of Meaning

This category relates particularly to the Gospel of John, where the author himself intends to convey, at times, two ideas with a single term. Actually, two of John's characteristics are complements of each other. One is the use of synonyms without significant difference. This is probably the case in the famous passage, John 21:15–17. It is well known that the Greek uses two different words for "love." Many sermons have been structured on the assumption that there is a significant difference between these words and that Peter was hurt when he heard the third question because Jesus used a less intensive word for "love." Given John's predilection for synonyms, however, it is more probable that the reason for his hurt was that Jesus repeated the question a third time, thereby reminding Peter of the three denials.

The other characteristic, which is the converse of the first, is the use of one word with two or more meanings. We see this most clearly in John 3:3–8, where Jesus speaks of being "born again." The Greek word ἄνωθεν also means "from above." This meaning, of course, is quite different from the diluted popular usage of the term, "born again," in the United States during the late 1970s.

Another example is the use of the word "blind" in John 9:39–41, where Jesus speaks with the Pharisees about their spiritual blindness following the healing of the physically blind man. There are two meanings of "rising" or "living again" found in the story of Jesus' raising of Lazarus (John 11:17–26). Likewise "lifted up" can refer both to the method of Jesus' crucifixion and to his ultimate glorification (John 3:14; 8:28; 12:32, 34). In each context, it is clear that the basic reference is to the crucifixion. However, it is striking that the word that John uses (ὑψόω) often has the meaning "exalt." This is seen in Acts 2:33 and in Philippians 2:9 (in the form ὑπερυψόω).

An extremely significant example of a double level of meaning is found in John's use of the word πιστεύω, "believe." To grasp the distinction in John will not only help us to understand that gospel, but also help us in our evangelistic efforts today. Because of the importance of the word, it is often assumed that a person who "believes" must be a true child of God. However, in John 2:23–25 we read that many people saw the miraculous signs that Jesus did in Jerusalem and "believed in his name." The text goes on, however, to imply that this was not what we would call "saving faith," because it says that "Jesus would not entrust himself to them, for he knew all men." This is reinforced by the words that follow, "he did not need man's testimony about man, for he knew what was in a man." The word "man" becomes a transition word to the beginning of what is now chapter 3, "now there was a man of the Pharisees named Nicodemus. . . ." Apparently John is showing at the end of our present chapter 2 that belief in Jesus may be only on a superficial level. Only Jesus knows what is in the heart of "man." John's primary example of a "man" who responded favorably to Jesus but who was not yet "born again" is Nicodemus.

This use of the word "believe" on two levels of meaning occurs again in John 8:27–41. "Even as he spoke, many put their faith in him" ("believed in him," v. 30). The next sentence is: "to the Jews who had believed in him, Jesus said, 'If you hold to my teaching you are really my disciples. Then you will know the truth, and the truth will set you free.'" The ensuing conversation reveals that these people did not "believe" in Jesus on the deeper level of saving faith. Actually, as the next paragraph, verses 42–47, makes clear, they still belonged to their "father, the devil." There is a serious need today to recognize that a person may "believe" the truth of the gospel of Christ prior to actual regeneration by the Holy Spirit. Failure to recognize this can result in great harm to people whom we claim have been converted before true "fruit" shows them to have been genuinely born again. Likewise recognition of this would help Christians who stumbled over the defection of someone who claimed to "believe," but who was never truly born again. James likewise uses "faith" with these two meanings in his famous passage on faith and works (James 2:14–26). The New International Version beautifully clarifies the meaning of that verse by translating λέγῃ not as "says," but as "claims," and ἡ πίστις not merely as "faith" but as "such faith."

The expositor will not find it easy to explain multiple levels of meaning to his congregation. He must do it in such a way that they are not unsettled in their assumption that Scripture is clear and straightforward. It needs to be shown that this is a legitimate literary method, and that such usage is usually made clear in the context.

Sensitive Issues

Perhaps this category has less justification in a book on exposition than it would in a regular book on homiletics, because it pertains not so much to the text as to the pastoral situation. It is worth mentioning, nevertheless. When we preach through the Bible, we inevitably come to some passages that deal with issues difficult to discuss in public. There are certain phrases in the Old Testament that are notorious for their frankness. Such is rarely the case in the New Testament. It is well, however, to be alert to words, expressions or doctrines that may come as a surprise or may be hard to accept. One example of this is Paul's use of the term σκύβαλα in Philippians 3:8. The word "rubbish" (NIV) is sufficient to get the idea across, but some preachers seem almost to relish the opportunity to introduce barnyard language at this point.

Another type of sensitive issue is the biblical teaching about hell. Unfortunately, many preachers avoid it altogether. What I plead for, however, is a sensitivity to the fact that descriptions of hell in terms of continual fire are so repulsive to people that they may turn off the message of the gospel completely. What is needed is a loving but frank explanation of what the Bible really teaches. It has been well said that we should not preach on hell unless we can do it (at least inwardly) with tears. Of course there is an "offense" to certain aspects of the Christian gospel. But poor semantics and sloppy pulpit dramatics can add to that offense by conveying a parody of hell, and not the truth that God wants to press on the hearts of humankind.

There are also certain teachings that are hyperbolic in nature, such as gouging out one's eye (Matthew 5:29), that need careful treatment lest they turn off someone who might think that Jesus was literally counseling such self-mutilation. Jesus' teaching about making oneself a eunuch (Matthew 19:12) likewise needs to be dealt with sensitively and with a clear explanation. I know one person who, sadly, took this literally and acted on it. We must always be sensitive to the thoughts and feelings of the congregation.

Apparent Discrepancies in the Gospels

Difficulties of this sort will be more acute for those who have studied the gospel parallels side by side than for those who simply read through one gospel at a time. Also many, if not most, seminary courses on the synoptic Gospels require study of a "synopsis of the Gospels" (which compares the Gospels word by word), rather than a "harmony" of the Gospels (which makes the comparison in larger units, thereby rendering verbal differences less conspicuous).

The preacher who has observed the differences revealed by a synoptic study and the preacher who even through the use a harmony has observed differences in order and in narrative differences need to remember that the average member of the congregation is probably unaware of these differences. At the same time, the preacher who has worked through synoptic difficulties to his own satisfaction, and, at the other extreme, the preacher who has never paid attention to such differences, both need to realize that there *may* be those in the congregation for whom these do constitute a problem. All of this is to say that this requires pastoral sensitivity as well as scholarly knowledge. The guidelines I would suggest are as follows: differences that are inconsequential to the purposes of the sermon and that are unlikely to be a problem to be already existing in the minds of the congregation, should not intrude into the sermon. Differences that are obvious or significant may require some comment. For example, when preaching on the cleansing of the temple in John, the preacher might say: "Many of you will have read a similar incident near the close of one of the other Gospels. It is not certain whether there were one or two such cleansings. In either case, it is appropriate for John to present this incident near the beginning of his gospel, because . . . (refer to the relevant themes in Johannine theology). Many Bible students think that there actually were two cleansings. Other Bible students, knowing that the gospel writers were sometimes led by the Holy Spirit to follow an order other than chronological for the sake of emphasis or for the grouping of similar topics, believe that the Spirit led John to put the cleansing of the temple prominently at the beginning of his gospel and the other writers to put it at the end. If any of you would like to discuss this interesting aspect of the study of the Gospels further, let me know and we'll arrange a talk."

In some churches even this may trouble some members of the congregation. Then it would be best to give an exposition of the cleansing of the temple in its context, making sure that the themes of the Johannine theology are clearly presented. The reason for its appearance at this point in the Gospel can certainly be explained without reference to the incident at the conclusion of the synoptic Gospels. If one of those passages is the subject of a sermon at some other time, it should be similarly expounded with reference to its own context and meaning.

A different problem occurs in the order of events following the triumphal entry of Jesus into Jerusalem. The sequence given by Matthew of Jesus' ministry in the temple and of his cursing of the fig tree is different from that given by Mark. It would serve no purpose to make an issue of this in the pulpit. However, something like this could be said: "Some of you may have observed that Mark appears to be following a strict chronological order when he writes down these events, while Matthew, in a way consistent with his more topical approach, groups the events surrounding Jesus teaching and the events surrounding the cursing of the fig tree separately. In this way the Holy Spirit has given us two perspectives on the same complex of events, one chronological and one topical."

A further example is found in the story about the centurion's servant in Matthew 8:5–13 and Luke 7:1–10. It appears that in Matthew the centurion went personally to see Jesus, whereas in Luke he sent servants. The perspective of Matthew is consistent with the custom of those days to receive an emissary of an official as though he were the official himself. This also has implications for apostleship, and it would not be at all strange if Matthew were thinking along these lines. In Luke, on the other hand, there is a great emphasis on the intimate connection between Christianity and Judaism. Luke frequently shows the oneness of spirit between pious Jews and pious Gentiles, both of whom tended to be open to the message of Jesus. There would be good reason for Luke to give the additional details that will show the piety of the centurion and the appreciation of this Gentile by the Jewish leaders. The preacher may not feel that such an explanation is appropriate for his congregation. In certain circumstances, however, with certain groups, such explanations can help people understand the contribution of each gospel.

In summary, on the one hand the pastor will not want to introduce topics that can be troublesome and that are too complex for resolution during the sermon. Even where it is not a terribly complex problem of synoptic relationships, he may not be able to spare the time even to introduce such an issue, if he is to give adequate treatment to the major teaching of the passage and its practical application. On the other hand, a preacher must never be guilty of ignoring or covering up features of the Gospels that are there by inspiration of the Holy Spirit and open for all to see.

My own suggestion is to preach the Gospels one by one in an expository series. For the most part this will not require reference to the other Gospels. When such reference would be useful as a means to showing the unique contribution of the Gospel under study in its portrait of Jesus and presentation of his teachings, this is certainly appropriate if done wisely. Matters that are merely issues of literary composition should for the most part be dealt with only in an appropriate situation, such as an advanced Bible study class, when there is ample time for thoroughness. Differences between the Gospels that are so obvious as to constitute a problem already for many in the congregation, or a potential problem, should be handled concisely, wisely, and in such a way as to fortify the congregation's confidence in the Scriptures.

One final suggestion regarding obscure passages in general. A good model is often better than a long explanation. If the obscurity is due to difficult Greek sentence structure or grammar, it may be wise to find a clear English translation that follows your own understanding of the text (I am assuming here a sufficient grasp of the Greek so that we can determine what is a satisfactory translation). The danger is that we merely choose a translation that fits our intuitive idea of what the passage means! In most cases the New International Version will offer the clearest translation. I gave an example of this earlier from Hebrews 1:4. Most people do not want to hear a long explanation; they just want to hear a meaning they can appropriate. In reading an alternate translation to the one we normally use, it is usually not wise to imply that the one we have been using is wrong at this point. This can shake confidence in the English text. It is better to say something like this: "I think the _____ Version has given the best English expression to the original meaning."

Chapter Ten

Praxis

Now that we have patiently worked through all this material together, how do we put it to practical use in constructing a sermon? A number of outlines have already been suggested on various passages. Now we shall take Romans 6:1–14 as a final example, and take the successive steps suggested in this book. The proportion of time spent on each step will vary according to our goals, the time available, and our facility in Greek. The English reader should be able to do most of this, but the student of Greek will certainly want to put that knowledge to use where appropriate.

Survey of the Context

Observe the Background

Of course the Book of Romans is so well known that we need not take time here to review the background of the book and of the argument thus far. In the pulpit we would do this. Even in an expository sermon we would assume that there are some without this understanding who have just begun attending the series.

Note the Immediate Context

We would explain the direction of thought and the conclusion to chapter 5, with its emphasis on grace. That conclusion also becomes the "connective tissue" along with 6:1, in particular the word "grace." We would explain why Paul felt it necessary to insist that grace was not a license to sin.

Dominant Characteristics and Themes

The initial words of the chapter introduce the problem of sin. But along with this verbal expression of a theme, there is a structural characteristic that must be observed if the passage is to be properly expounded. It is a series of rhetorical questions that extend beyond our passage, in 6:1; 6:15; 7:7; and 7:13. These are mentioned below under patterns. It is this series of questions that gives shape to the whole section of Romans 6 and 7.

Practical Exegesis

There are a number of items in this passage that are significant enough for special attention during my preparatory study. We need not list all of them here, but certainly there are several that claim special attention. Terms like "sin" and "grace" will probably have already been explained during the course of an exposition on Romans. New terms like "died to sin" and "baptized into Christ Jesus" (and "baptized into his death") will require explanation now. The phrase, "count yourselves dead to sin" cries out for interpretation; it will certainly be difficult for the congregation to understand. All of these terms are important doctrinally, thematically in Romans, and, in this passage, important ethically as well.

Exegetical Outline

The following lays out the text in paragraph form. I am using the English text (NIV), but am consulting the Greek to see if I want to make any modifications.

v. 1   What shall we say, then?
Shall we go on sinning
    so that grace may increase?

v. 2   By no means!
    (we) who died to sin
How shall we live in it any longer?

v. 3   Or don't you know
    that all of us . . .
      who were baptized into Christ Jesus
    . . . were baptized into his death?

v. 4   We were therefore buried with him
      through baptism
      into death
    in order that . . .
      just as Christ was raised from the dead
        through the glory of the Father,
    . . . we too may live a new life.

v. 5   If we have been united with him
                in his death
        we will certainly also be united with him
                in his resurrection.
v. 6   For we know
            that our old self was crucified with him
                so that the body of sin might be rendered powerless,
                    that we should no longer be slaves to sin—
v. 7   because anyone who has died has been freed from
                    sin.
v. 8   (Now)
            if we died with Christ
        we believe
            that we will also live with him
v. 9   For we know that . . .
                since Christ was raised from the dead,
                he cannot die again,
                death no longer has mastery over him.
v. 10   The death . . .
            (which) he died,
        . . . he died to sin once for all;
        But the life . . .
            (which) he lives,
        . . . he lives to God.
v. 11   In the same way, count yourselves
            dead to sin
            but alive to God in Christ Jesus.
v. 12   Therefore, do not let sin reign in your mortal body
            so that you obey its evil desires.
v. 13   Do not offer the parts of your body to sin
                as instruments of sin
        but rather offer yourselves to God
                as those who have returned from death to life;
        and offer the parts of your body to him
                as instruments of righteousness.
v. 14   For sin shall not be your master
            for you are not under law
            but under grace.

Patterns in the Text

Narrative patterns

None.

Compositional Patterns

There are several strong contrasts as the passage moves along, between life and death, and then between offering ourselves to sin and offering ourselves to God. There is comparison as well, pointed out by the words, "just as" and "we too" in verse 4. Repetition is seen first of all in the overall pattern observed earlier in chapters 5 and 6, the series of four questions, "What shall we say then? Shall we go sinning. . . ?" (6:1); "What then? Shall we sin because. . . ?" (6:15); "What shall we say, then? Is the law sin?" (7:7); and "Did that which is good, then, become death to me?" (7:13). There is also a repetition of key terms and ideas here, such as death and life; "united with him," in verse 5; "into" three times in verses 3 and 4; "body" in verses 12 and 13, and so on. There is a climax in verse 14. There is cruciality in the Resurrection, which marks here the change from sin, death, and bondage to obedience, life, and freedom. Cause to effect is seen in the effect the death and resurrection of Christ have in our lives. There is a constant interchange between the experience of Christ and the experience of Christians. An example of substantiation is found in verse 9: "for we know . . . ," as well as in the climax, verse 14, "For sin shall not be your master. . . ."

Semantic Patterns

Some of the foregoing compositional patterns are based on semantic patterns, such as the contrast between "life" and "death." These also form semantic fields, such as the whole area of living and dying, or that of oldness and newness. Some of these are overlapping in their significance. For example, "resurrection" is part of the semantic field of living and dying, along with "death," "died," "dead," "buried," "raised," and "life." But "resurrection" also is connected with the idea of newness in verse 4, "live a new life." There are reversives: Christ died, Christ lives; we have been united with him in his death, we have been united with him in his resurrection; "do not give the parts of your body as slaves to sin, but give them as slaves to righteousness." There is also a reciprocal idea here, both expressed and understood, for example, "dead to sin but alive to God" (v. 11). Some of these examples are also equivalents, "united with him in his death/resurrection," "died/live with Christ," "buried/raised with Christ," "slavery to sin/righteousness." There are also several terms in the same semantic field that are likely to be overlooked because they are in different parts of speech, for example, terms for purpose, that include the Greek particle, ἵνα ("in order that"), and the articular infinitive of purpose, τοῦ μηκέτι δουλεύειν ("that we should no longer be slaves").

Final Touches

We should also be aware of the emotional "color pattern" in this passage. There is a strong sense of shock and concern here, indicated by the expression, "By no means!" (μὴ γένοιτο). The rhetorical questions just observed also provide a feeling of challenge and urgency. We need to look for any significant deep structure. Perhaps the most obvious example is in verse 3. The words, "who were baptized into Christ Jesus" are, in what grammarians call the "surface structure," the relative form of "We were baptized into Christ Jesus." But that statement requires explanation. It is necessary, therefore, to make sure that the congregation knows what it means to be baptized into Christ before they can understand the sentence that contains this relative clause. Last, we need to summarize the passage in a single sentence: We should not continue living a sinful life, because just as surely as Christ ended his life on earth by death and rose to begin a new life, so, morally, we have died to our old life and should, as those raised with Christ to a new life, yield ourselves completely to God.

Function and Application

We now turn to the function and application of the passage. In its original context, it was designed to prevent a misunderstanding of the doctrine of grace. The readers were for the most part people whom Paul had not met. He did not have assurance that they would understand the need of identification with Christ in his death and resurrection unless he explained this to them. The results he sought are easily discernible both in his argument and in his use of imperatives in verses 11–13. The function might be described in several ways: (1) motivational, because of Paul's strong emotional tone, indicating a sense of urgency; (2) dealing with doctrinal issues, to the extent that he is vindicating the Christian idea of grace; (3) showing a cause-effect relationship in the effect that the death and resurrection of Christ should have in our lives; (4) laying a foundation for action, especially in the statement of verse 14, but also in a general way; (5) teaching ethics. No specific situations are described, but a foundation for holy living is certainly provided. There is a small book on this section of Romans, written many years ago by Dr. J. Oliver Buswell, Jr., the title of which is somewhat quaint, but nevertheless appropriate: "Why a Christian Does Not Lead a Wicked Life." If we modify this somewhat for a contemporary audience, perhaps by substituting the word "sinful" for "wicked," we can answer the question posed either by moving down the passage itself point by point, using the paragraph outline as a guide, or we can take the various patterns we have discovered, and draw on the entire passage under several main headings, stressing (1) union with Christ in his death, (2) union with Christ in his resurrection, and (3) the decisions called for in the final paragraph. The last sentence is, as we observed, both foundational and climatic, and can form the conclusion to our sermon, whether as part of the final point, as a separate point in itself, or perhaps in conjunction with an appropriate concluding illustration.

With this selection of functions, it becomes very important to understand the need of the congregation. With new believers, it might be best to devote a good deal of time and emphasis to the doctrinal aspects of the passage, so the new Christian can understand the nature of grace and the basis of Christian morality. With Christians who do not show a strong concern for moral living, the tone of the sermon might become more hortatory and motivational. If the pastor thinks that there are ethical problems due to a lack of understanding concerning the relationship between the gospel and the Christian life, he might stress the foundational aspects of this passage.

Is this a difficult text? I think so, because of the concept of being baptized into Christ and his death, which might not be understood by many in the congregation because of such phrases as "old self" in verse 6 and "the body of sin" in the same verse, and because of the seemingly mysterious phrase, "count yourselves dead to sin," in verse 11. There is a great danger that because some of the phrases in this passage are so common in Christian parlance, the preacher might not realize how much teaching he will have to do if the congregation is to understand and apply the message.

Homiletical Form

What shape should my sermon take? What should be the main characteristics? What impressions should remain with the congregation? To what point of action should they be brought? How can this fit into an expository series on Romans?

To take the last question first, I would work carefully from the doctrine of justification by grace taught in Romans 1–4. (I should also be watching any trajectories of terms throughout Romans.) Commentators differ widely as to whether chapter 5 belongs with the preceding or the following sections in Romans. I see 5:1–11 as a summary of how things stand as a result of justification: we have peace, joy, and hope (see my earlier outlines on this passage). Romans 5:12–19 introduces an important aspect of Paul's view of the life and work of Christ: a parallel between Adam and Christ. This prepares us for Romans 6 in two ways. (1) We are strongly conscious of two worlds, the world of Adam, a sphere of death, and the world of Christ, a sphere of life. Therefore, when Paul talks in chapter 6 about death and life, we are ready to see the implication: the person united with Christ shares his new life, and is done with the old syndrome of sin and death. This theme continues through Romans 8. (2) The reference to grace in 5:20–21 is a springboard, as we have seen, to the issue of implications for our moral life.

I would certainly use the four questions in 6:1; 6:15; 7:7 and 7:13 as a framework for my series on this part of Romans. I would involve the congregation in a quest for the answer, making sure that I apply these questions, originally meaningful to a Jewish Christian concerned with the Law, to a contemporary congregation.

I would make use of the equivalents, repeated words and phrases, comparisons and contrasts either by structuring main or sub-points on these, or by introducing them again and again by way of reinforcement in the sermon. I would present the congregation with the issue of choice and lead them step by step to the exhortation in verses 11–13.

The conclusion in verse 14 ought to be presented both as a climax and as the definitive answer to the question of verse 1. While the inner verses show how and why the Christian "does not lead a wicked life" in terms of identification with Christ, the concluding verse emphasizes the result in terms of the transition from law to grace. (Note the strong contrast between ὑπὸ νόμον, "under law," and ὑπὸ χάριν, "under grace".) Under the law one was condemned, and, since the law could not effect freedom from sin (as Paul is showing in chapters 6 and 7), one was under the bondage of sin. But grace releases us from that bondage and, because of the resurrection power of Christ, opens the way to a new life of true obedience to God.

Because the problem of sin is deeply troubling to most religious people, and because of the strong emotional color in this passage, the conclusion to my sermon should not be a dry doctrinal summary, but should contain almost an impassioned note of affirmation. I believe that a sermon on this passage should have the same characteristics as the passage itself: a combination of doctrinal clarity and concern with personal application. The contemporary audience, like the original readers of Romans, should be brought to a point of yieldedness, commitment, and obedience.

The actual structure can take many forms. If I follow the paragraph outline, I will select from the large number of main and subordinate clauses those few that will faithfully represent the flow of the passage. There is a discernible progress marked with words having to do with our *understanding*. Note the following analysis:

> Some questions to ponder: "What shall we say then . . . shall we sin . . . (or, if we died to sin) how can we live in it any longer?" (vv. 1, 2).
> Some facts to know: "Don't you know" (v. 3); "For we know" (v. 5).
> Something to believe: "We believe . . ." (v. 8).
> Something to count on: "Count yourselves . . ." (v. 11).

Rather than follow the paragraph sequentially, I may choose to work in a circular fashion, that is to center on each of the affirmations about death, life, and the decisions called for, coming back to these at each point they occur in the text. Actually, Paul himself worked in a circular fashion. Although the text proceeds logically, the topics themselves are repeated in differing form again and again. I might center primarily on the question, "What does it mean to be united with Christ?" since that is a key idea. The term, "united" occurs in a significant "equivalent" structure, which also contains a reversive: "united with him in his death . . . united with him in his resurrection." Therefore I can say that:

> Being united with Christ means being dead to the old life.
> Being united with Christ means being alive to a new life.
> Being united to Christ means being committed to a new way of life.

A totally different approach would be to begin with the opening questions and build a strong sense of concern and anticipation, give a clear exposition of verses 3–10, and then devote the latter part of the sermon to application. In this case I would suggest *two* outlines: a logical content outline for the exposition, and then an outline of verses 11–14 in order to give a compelling exhortation. This "concluding" outline might be structured around the imperatives of verses 11–14 as follows:

"Count yourselves . . ." (λογίζεσθε ἑαυτοὺς) v. 11
"Do not let sin reign . . ." (μὴ . . . βασιλευέτω) v. 12
"Do not offer . . ." (μηδὲ παριστάνετε) v. 13
"But offer . . ." (ἀλλά παραστήσατε) v.13

This kind of "double outline" could be very awkward and confusing to the congregation if not handled well. One advantage of it is that it follows the content and the mood of the text, properly appropriating the two functions of doctrine and ethical exhortation. I would probably try to integrate the two outlines by using indirect exposition. That is, I would develop a primary outline that includes the opening questions in the chapter and the closing exhortations, with the exposition of verses 3–13 as the central element. Here is a possible outline that includes several ideas presented above:

Theme: Making the most of God's grace.
Lead in: We make the most of God's grace by:
1. Rejecting the tendency to presume on God's grace (vv. 1–2).
2. Understanding our new life in Christ (vv. 3–10) (exposition).
3. Yielding ourselves to God ("Count yourselves," etc.).

This variety of possibilities may come as a disappointment to those who may have been expecting a single neat sermon outline on Romans 6. But this book has attempted to be honest and vigorous in dealing with the real complexities of sermon preparation. To be sure, an example could have been chosen that yielded a simple obvious outline. Some have been presented earlier. But that is not "life in the study." Neither is it "life in the parish." The meaning of the text is univocal, but its presentation and its application can be as varied as the literary style of the biblical authors, the preaching style of the pastor, and the needs of the contemporary congregation.

The Preaching Program

One final factor in the structuring of a sermon, which I have

One final factor in the structuring of a sermon, which I have reserved for last, is the larger environment of the sermon: the preaching program.

How long a series should one plan for a single book of the Bible? Some preachers have successfully preached for more than a year on one book. This testifies to the richness of God's Word. Yet there are dangers. Unless one enlarges on minor topics imbedded in the text, the congregation will not be exposed to a healthy variety of doctrines. It might be better to stress the main teachings of the book, finish the series, and get on to other books. Actually, it is better to teach a doctrine from a book that features it, as we have seen, than to squeeze it out of a passing comment in a text on another topic.

In planning a series, we certainly want to consider the spiritual and personal needs of the congregation. The choice of books and topics should, like the individual sermon, come both from "above" and from "below," with Scripture and need meeting in the pulpit.

The year's preaching program should include (assuming, for the moment, that most of our messages will be expository), a balance of books not only from the Old and New Testaments, but also from the different types of literature in the Bible, for example, historical, proverbial, psalms, doctrinal, and so forth. Decisions concerning the preaching program as a whole are no less demanding than the decision as to what to preach on a given Sunday. Yet this decision is rendered somewhat easier when I plan ahead to include a variety of messages on a number of needs and topics. One can choose more thoughtfully and objectively when not pressed by the need of a topic to put in the bulletin by Wednesday! (Also we have much more time to gather relevant resource material when we plan ahead.) All this can be integrated with the church year.

At the same time, it is not merely pious talk to remind ourselves how important it is to depend prayerfully on the Lord for his guidance in choosing topics and passages, whether one week or six months ahead. Also we should be flexible to change when circumstances and the leading of the Spirit so indicate. There is nothing sacred about an unbroken continuity. In fact, a congregation will sense the urgency of a message even more keenly when the pastor considers it important enough to interrupt his series.

Planning for other occasions, especially Bible conferences, requires other considerations. Like it or not, we must realize that people attending a summer camp or conference are there for relaxation and entertainment. I see no reason why one cannot combine rich Bible teaching with a warm and cheerful spirit. One must paint with a larger brush, for details may easily be lost due to distractions, such as children, birds, and weather. The series must be self-contained, and the conferees should leave with several clear concepts and imperatives in their minds and hearts. Perhaps narratives, parables, and character studies are better choices in some situations than didactic passages. Because sessions are closer together, usually once a day, there can be a better carry-over of ideas and impressions. At the same time, concentration will probably be poorer than in church. Also there may be those who, in the absence of pew Bibles, listen without following in the text. Everything should be clearly explained and illustrated. People should leave encouraged and refreshed, happy to have heard the Word of God.

In fact, that is my hope for all those who hear our expositions of God's Word. Except for the occasionally needed severe sermon, may our messages fill people with joy, peace, and hope.

And while this has been a book on methodology, may we remember that it is only by the Spirit of God, acting in sovereign grace and power and working through our prayers, that our sermons will have any spiritual effect.

Notes

1. James W. Sire, *Scripture Twisting: Twenty Ways the Cults Misread the Bible* (Downers Grove: InterVarsity, 1980).

2. Among the better known books on hermeneutics are Milton S. Terry, *Biblical Hermeneutics* (1883; reprint, Grand Rapids: Zondervan, 1969); Bernard Ramm, *Protestant Biblical Interpretation,* 3d ed. (Grand Rapids: Baker, 1970); A. Berkeley Mickelsen, *Interpreting the Bible* (Grand Rapids: Eerdmans, 1963). Two works dealing with special issues and particular books or passages are: I. H. Marshall, ed., *New Testament Interpretation* (Grand Rapids: Eerdmans, 1977) and Morris A. Inch and Hassell Bullock, eds., *The Literature and Meaning of Scripture* (Grand Rapids: Baker, 1981). For a combination of hermeneutical and exegetical guidelines toward the structuring of a sermon, the finest book a preacher could find, and unique in the field, is Walter C. Kaiser, Jr., *Toward an Exegetical Theology: Biblical Exegesis for Preaching and Teaching* (Grand Rapids: Baker, 1981).

3. The finest work on this subject is Anthony C. Thiselton, *The Two Horizons: New Testament Hermeneutics and Philosophical Description* (Grand Rapids: Eerdmans, 1980). The seminal study, with which Thiselton interacts, Hans-Georg Gadamer, *Truth and Method* (London: Sheed and Ward, 1975), was originally published as *Warheit und Methode, Grundzüge einer philosophischen Hermeneutik* (Tübingen: Mohr, 1965).

4. The reader should be aware that there is a good deal of disagreement as to the application of contemporary sociological methodology to the New Testament period. Some books that appear to be objective descriptions of New Testament background are actually presenting for consideration by other scholars, particular approaches to sociological approaches. Such "probings" include the following: Gerd Theissen, *Sociology of Early Palestinian Christianity* (Philadelphia: Fortress, 1978); Howard Clark Kee, *Christian Origins in Sociological Perspective* (Philadelphia: Westminster, 1980); and Bruce J. Malina, *The New Testament World: Insights from Cultural Anthropology* (Atlanta: John Knox, 1981). Scholarly works on the historical background include Martin Hengel's massive work, *Judaism and Hellenism* (English translation; Philadelphia: Fortress, 1974) and the two-volume scholarly (non-evangelical) *Introduction to the New Testament* by Helmut Koester, the first volume of which, *History, Culture and Religion*

of the Hellenistic Age (Philadelphia: Fortress, 1982) is a detailed study of the period. Hengel has some very useful shorter studies, including *Property and Riches in the Early Church* (Philadelphia: Fortress, 1974) and *Crucifixion* (Philadelphia: Fortress, 1977). Two works on Jerusalem, one by Joachim Jeremias, *Jerusalem in the Time of Jesus* (Philadelphia: Fortress, 1969) and John Wilkinson, *Jerusalem as Jesus Knew It* (London: Thames and Hudson, 1978) typify the kind of information available for the student of the Gospels. Various aspects of New Testament history are illuminated by A. N. Sherwin-White, *Roman Society and Roman Law in the New Testament*, The Sarum Lectures 1960-1961 (Oxford: Clarendon Press, 1963). A very informative book on daily life in biblical times, with much rich illustration for sermons, is to be reissued by Moody Press under the authorship of Walter L. Liefeld and Grant Osborne, *Manners and Customs of Bible Lands.*

5. We now have a wealth of Bible encyclopedias and dictionaries. The most comprehensive evangelical work presently available as I write is the five-volume *The Zondervan Pictorial Encyclopedia of the Bible*, edited by Merrill C. Tenney (1975). The revision of the *International Standard Bible Encyclopedia*, edited by Geoffrey Bromily, is currently in process of publication by Eerdmans. A three-volume encyclopedia, the *Illustrated Bible Dictionary*, published in 1980 by Tyndale, is an enlarged form of the *New Bible Dictionary*, the revised edition of which was published by Tyndale in 1982. The diagrams, maps, and illustrations in this work are the most graphic and helpful I have seen.

6. Charles Talbert, *Literary Patterns, Theological Themes and the Genre of Luke-Acts*, Society of Biblical Literature Monograph Series 20 (Missoula: Scholars Press, 1974).

7. Gerhard Kittel and Gerhard Friedrich, eds., *Theological Dictionary of the New Testament*, Geoffrey Bromily, trans., 10 vols. (Grand Rapids: Eerdmans, 1964-76).

8. Colin Brown, ed., *The New International Dictionary of New Testament Theology*, 3 vols. (Grand Rapids: Zondervan, 1975-78).

9. F. Blass and A. Debrunner, *A Greek Grammar of the New Testament*, Robert W. Funk, trans. and ed. (Chicago: University of Chicago Press, 1961).

10. James Hope Moulton, *A Grammar of New Testament Greek*, vol. 3 (Edinburgh: T. & T. Clark, 1963).

11. A. T. Robertson, *Grammar of the Greek New Testament in the Light of Historical Research* (Nashville: Broadman, 1923).

12. Bruce M. Metzger, *A Textual Commentary of the Greek New Testament*, (London and New York: United Bible Societies, 1971).

13. Merrill C. Tenney, *Galatians: The Charter of Christian Liberty* (Grand Rapids: Eerdmans, 1950).

14. Irving L. Jensen, *Independent Bible Study* (Chicago: Moody, 1963).

15. Johannes P. Louw, "Discourse Analysis and the Greek New Testament" *Bible Translator* 24 (1973): 101–18.

16. Examples of a structuralistic approach to biblical literature are frequently found in the periodical *Seimeia*. Vols. 1 and 2 (both 1974) and 9 (1977) provide examples from the study of the parables. Assessments of the value of this approach vary, and structuralists have been modifying their own methodology. It is not yet at a point where the average busy pastor can easily select the good from that which is marginal or useless.

17. Robert A. Traina, *Methodical Bible Study* (New York: Ganis and Harris, 1952).

18. Jensen, *Independent Bible Study* (cf. footnote 14).

19. Richard Chenevix Trench, *Synonyms of the New Testament*, 9th ed. (1880; reprint Grand Rapids: Eerdmans, 1966).

20. C. E. B. Cranfield, *A Critical and Exegetical Commentary on the Epistle to the Romans*. International Critical Commentary, 2d series (Edinburgh: T. & T. Clark, 1975), pp. 264f.

21. John C. Hawkins, *Horae Synopticae* (Grand Rapids: Baker, 1968).

22. Robert Morgenthaler, *Statistik des Neutestamentlichen Wortschatzes* (Zürich: Gotthelf, 1973).

23. Lloyd Gaston, *Horae Synopticae Electronicae: Word Statistics of the Synoptic Gospels* (Missoula: Scholars Press, Society of Biblical Literature, 1973).

24. Lloyd M. Perry, *Biblical Preaching for Today's World* (Chicago: Moody, 1973), pp. 70, 147.

25. The concern to bridge the world of the Bible and the contemporary world finds eloquent expression in a work that has appeared since I wrote this chapter, *Between Two Worlds*, by John R. W. Stott (Grand Rapids: Eerdmans, 1982). It will undoubtedly take its place as one of the most significant of all books on preaching. See especially chapter 4, "Preaching as Bridge Building," pp. 135–79.

26. Lloyd M. Perry, *Biblical Preaching for Today's World*, chapter 5, "Biblical Preaching and Life-Situation Preaching," especially pp. 116f., 119–21.

27. Sidney Greidanus, *Sola Scriptura. Problems and Principles in Preaching Historical Texts* (Toronto: Wedge, 1970).

28. Henry Grady Davis, *Design for Preaching* (Philadelphia: Fortress, 1958), pp. 139–62.

29. Haddon W. Robinson, *Biblical Preaching: The Development and Delivery of Expository Messages* (Grand Rapids: Baker, 1980).

30. Lloyd M. Perry, *Biblical Sermon Guide* (Grand Rapids: Baker, 1970).

31. Perry, *Sermon Guide*, p. 63.

32. Perry, *Sermon Guide*, pp. 27-60.

33. Robinson, *Biblical Preaching*, p. 125.

34. S. J. Schultz and M. A. Inch, *Interpreting the Word of God* (Chicago: Moody, 1976), pp. 105–27.

35. There are many books on parables which are helpful for preaching. A recent work that summarizes much of the best of previous studies is Robert Stein, *An Introduction to the Parables of Jesus* (Philadelphia: Westminster, 1981). Two books by Kenneth E. Bailey provide especially interesting cultural information: *Poet and Peasant* (1976) and *Through Peasant Eyes* (1980). Both are published by Eerdmans.

36. Mickelsen, *Interpreting the Bible*, 179–235. This work and others on hermeneutics are listed in note 2.

37. Richard Soulen, *Handbook of Biblical Criticism*, 2d ed. (Atlanta: John Knox, 1980).

38. See also the issue of subjectivism and objectivism discussed in Greidanus, *Sola Scriptura*.

39. D. A. Carson, *The King James Version Debate* (Grand Rapids: Baker, 1979).

Bibliography

Of the many books touching on expository preaching, the following will probably be of the greatest help in conjunction with the guidelines we have proposed.

Davis, Henry Grady, *Design for Preaching* (Philadelphia: Fortress, 1958)

Kaiser, Walter C., Jr., *Toward an Exegetical Theology: Biblical Exegesis for Preaching and Teaching* (Grand Rapids: Baker, 1981).

Koller, Charles W., *Expository Preaching Without Notes* (Grand Rapids: Baker, 1962).

Perry, Lloyd M., *Biblical Sermon Guide* (Grand Rapids: Baker, 1970).

_____ and Sell, Charles M., *Speaking to Life's Problems* (Chicago: Moody Press, 1983).

Robinson, Haddon W., *Biblical Preaching: The Development and Delivery of Expository Messages* (Grand Rapids: Baker, 1980).

Stott, John R. W., *Between Two Worlds: The Art of Preaching in the Twentieth Century* (Grand Rapids: Eerdmans, 1982).

Some other general works mentioned in this book that are especially useful are:

Brown, Colin, ed., *The New International Dictionary of New Testament Theology*, 3 vols. (Grand Rapids: Zondervan, 1975-78).

Inch, A., and Bullock, Hassell, eds., *The Literature and Meaning of Scripture* (Grand Rapids: Baker, 1981).

Jensen, Irving L., *Independent Bible Study* (Chicago: Moody Press, 1963).

Kittel, Gerhard, and Friedrich, Gerhard, eds., *Theological Dictionary of the New Testament,* Geoffrey Bromily, trans., 10 vols. (Grand Rapids: Eerdmans, 1964-76).

Marshall, I. H., ed., *New Testament Interpretation* (Grand Rapids: Eerdmans, 1977).

Mickelsen, A. Berkeley, *Interpreting the Bible* (Grand Rapids: Eerdmans, 1963).

Ramm, Bernard, *Protestant Biblical Interpretation,* 3rd ed. (Grand Rapids: Baker, 1970).

Terry, Milton S., *Biblical Hermeneutics* (1883; reprint, Grand Rapids: Zondervan, l969).

Thiselton, Anthony C., *The Two Horizons: New Testament Hermeneutics and Philosophical Description* (Grand Rapids: Eerdmans, 1980).

Traina, Robert A., *Methodical Bible Study* (New York: Ganis and Harris, 1952).

The following excellent textbook on exegesis appeared after this book was completed:

Fee, Gordon D., *New Testament Exegesis: A Handbook for Students and Pastors* (Philadelphia: Westminster, 1983).

For a full bibliography:

Litfin, A. Duane, and Robinson, Haddon W., *Recent Homiletical Thought. An Annotated Bibliography,* vol. 2, 1966-79 (Grand Rapids: Baker, 1983).

Author Index

General Index

Scripture Index

SCRIPTURE INDEX